MR. MANN, MY TEACHER

Perry Mann is a teacher, writer, philosopher, naturalist, and lawyer. At 90 he works his two gardens in Summers County, West Virginia, and does a little "lawyering" as he calls it.

After serving his country in World War II, he went to Washington and Lee on the G.I. Bill graduating with honors. Later he went to the University of Virginia for his Master in Education and in 1971 returned to Washington and Lee for his law degree. He taught in public schools grades 6-12 and at Concord College until hanging out his attorney sign at his office in Hinton, West Virginia, where he is a partner with his daughter today.

Having written thousands of articles for various publications, his work is well known by many, but this book is the first to present some of his work in one volume.

Our story is one for a novella itself. He was my high school English teacher, and his effect on me was profound. It has been said it takes only a few good teachers to change a life forever, and he was mine. I went off to college because of him and became a teacher because of him. I lost track of him, but I never quit talking about him to my own children and my students throughout the years. When I rediscovered him in May of 2011, I wrote him, and we have been in daily contact since. When I told my family I wanted to publish this book, my son asked why this book and why now.

This moment is the right time for this book because our planet is in trouble, and Perry Mann's words, descriptions, and ideas remind us of the gift of and the necessity for nature in our lives. He was chosen as one of fifty Americans who tell the truth and was featured in Robert Shetterly's book of the same title, and his connection to nature through his gardens and mountains is the substance of his truth. He is an amazing man and a treasure.

Thanks to my sons, Matthew and Nicholas, and my husband who believed in Mr. Mann and me and who drove this project forward. They too are my heroes. Sarah Harford Bullus, Katie Rice Baker, and Joseph Hamilton Ball, former classmates, also encouraged me onward. This great man touched their lives, and they too never forgot.

MANN & NATURE

Published by Kettle Moraine Publishing co

Cover portrait by Robert Shetterly

Cover design by Nicholas Bowers

Photographs by Perry Mann

Printed by Rockford Litho Center

Printed on Recycled Paper

To Ann Farrell Bowers without whose enthusiasm
and work this book would not be and to Michael
Ferrell and Mae Bowers and all children with hope
they will always have wild places where they can
explore, play, and dream.

ORIGIN OF MANN

Spring

SUMMER

FALL

WINTER

LEGACY

1

The Gift of Poverty

A history professor who was never asked to give a commencement address had a dream of what he would say to mark the occasion to the class of 2000 had he been asked. He dreamed he would tell them he wanted to talk to them about the graduation gift their parents did not give them.

"The present that you've been cheated of, members of the class of 2000, is poverty. Not so much the actuality of going hungry and worrying where the rent money is going to come from, but a living memory of such experiences."

He would remind them their grandparents passed from adolescence to adulthood during the Great Depression. "No matter how financially secure your grandfathers and grandmothers afterwards might have become, for the most part they still measured life against the mental template set in the 1930s."

I am one of those fortunates who were not cheated of the gift of poverty. I didn't ask for it; in fact, I wasn't even aware poverty was what I got. It just came to me inexplicably and almost overnight. I remember, however, the beginning of its coming.

When members of this generation read in the history books that in March of 1933 President Roosevelt declared a bank holiday from which thousands of banks never opened their doors again, they have no conception of the scope of the reversal of fortunes resulting from that event. But, I remember well the morning of the holiday and of my father, who was a loan officer at the Security Bank and Trust Co., leaving for work and telling my mother he would rather die than go to the bank that morning. He knew his bank was insolvent, and for him and millions of others the end of the great prosperity of the Roaring Twenties had come, and the Great Depression, when the gift of poverty came willy-nilly to a third of this nation's people, had begun.

My father did not need the gift of poverty, for he knew poverty from day one of his life until after World War I when he left the farm and went to the city to seek his fortune. The lessons of poverty rather than an education helped him to rise to middle class status by 1929 when he and many others had to pay for their hubris and a misplaced faith and security in the miracles of capitalism and in the marvels of the city.

The prosperity of the twenties lured millions of youth to town, but the Depression of the thirties forced as many to return to the land and to their parents' farms from which they had left with high hopes. My father did not return; he toughed it out. But I went back to live much of my life with my grandparents who by any tangible measure were poor. And it was on that farm with them where I gained the gift of poverty, a gift that was many-sided.

First, I learned to work, work that was physical, needful, and done out-of-doors under the sky and clouds with the sun and breeze. I learned just how much a person can do with muscle and sweat and how long he can endure laboring in a day. My grandfather's day was 5:00 A. M. to 6:00 P.M., earlier and later if exigencies arose, and my grandmother's an hour or more earlier and later, and I was at their sides most of those hours. I have put in ten hours in the hay field in 95 degrees and spent a good part of those hours in a barn loft throwing back hay pitched to me from a wagon. When I hear a person who works in an air-conditioned office say he has worked hard that day, I think of how watered down the word work has become.

I learned the value of family, of a stable family, a predictable family and a family who worked together for survival. There was a division of labor; everyone had his or her work responsibilities. Monday for the women was washday and Tuesday ironing day. I remember the blued sheets bright with sun at play with the wind, and the bib overalls hanging like scare-crows on the clothesline. Then on the next day Grandmother or Aunt Sadie stood before the wood-fired cook stove ironing every item from the clothesline with irons heated on the stove and touched to a waxed cloth for free sliding.

For the women everyday was meal day. Three of them were prepared in winter from scratch or from what was canned, salted, buried, or stored. With no prepared foods or refrigeration, each meal was from beginning. And what meals! It was around the table at breakfast, dinner and supper, winter and summer, that much of the joy of rural poverty was shared. The rewards of work materialized in the form of oatmeal with cream, fried ham and red-eye gravy, lard biscuits, applesauce, milk, butter, jellies, and at dinner and supper green beans, tomatoes, fried potatoes, sausage, cucumbers in cream, corn-on-the-cob, corn bread, cakes, and pies.

My grandfather's work was outside. He fed the stock and sharpened the hoes before he called to me to get up. We were in the fields or in the woods by 6:00 A.M. In summer it was plowing and hoeing corn; cutting, raking, shocking, and hauling hay; cutting wheat with a cradle, shocking it, and bringing in the sheaves to await the coming of the thrashing machine, an occasion that was the harvesting and social event of the season. Neighbors met at a designated household to thrash and then to have the noon meal: what a memorable combination of cheer and chaff!

In the fall and winter, it was getting in the wood for heat for fireplace and stove. It was cleaning out fence corners, feeding the stock, bringing home the lambs, hunting the squirrel, rabbit, and quail, and sitting before the fire in long, dark evenings with roasting shins and shivering shoulders.

I learned nature first hand. I never saw a bird new to me that I didn't ask my grandfather the name of it. He had a name for all of them. The names were not as in the books, but they were close. He called a phoebe a peewee and a killdeer a killdee and a towhee a cherree. It was the same for the trees. I hunted and fished and trapped. I had a dog that was at my side the minute I left the house, staying there until I went in. We roamed the woods together spending afternoons digging in the earth and moving a ton of rocks to get at some holed-up varmint.

I learned community and communal cooperation. When Arnold Epling came down with sickness in the fall and couldn't get his winter wood in, the neighbors came one day and did it for him. I was one of them pulling one end of a crosscut saw. When Mrs. Houchin lay on her death bed, my grandmother was there attending her when she took her last breath. I heard it. When hay was down and wet weather was threatening, neighbors came to get the hay up before the rain. Always when death or sickness befell a household, the neighbors were there. And when there were weddings and births and baptisms, everyone around came to celebrate.

I was sent by my family to help paint the church as its donation toward that project. On more than one occasion of death, I with my buddies Punk and Bob dug graves for the deceased at the church cemetery the old-fashioned way with pick and shovel and donated our labor to the family of the bereaved. And we were on the church grounds helping ourselves to fried chicken and potato salad on those days of all-day preaching with dinner on the grounds.

Once Uncle John Carden sent out a distress call: he had hay down ready to put up, and rain was imminent. Could someone come and help on the Fourth of July for a few hours? Punk and I, who had planned a fishing foray for the day, were chosen to go. The few hours turned into nine hours. We didn't finish getting in the hay until 3:30 P.M., but with ninety cents each for the work and a few hours left of the day, we went fishing anyway.

The poverty I speak of was country poverty, not street poverty, not the pernicious kind of idleness on concrete. The poverty I remember and lived was of no money, mostly barter and trade but little exchange with cash. Some eggs and butter were sold. Cream was skimmed and collected in a metal container and, when full, taken to the train station and sent off to Baltimore from where a check was cut and sent back to help pay the mortgage.

The Great World War II brought an end to it. The boys of the Depression by the millions left the farms and the cities, and in uniforms they became the Greatest Generation, or so they have been called. I never felt great, but I was there, and I am happy to say that I reaped the rewards of the gift of poverty.

2

THE TRAUMA OF TRANSPLANTATION

It's common knowledge among mountain people a rabbit when jumped and chased will circle back to the proximity of its nest. This habit is often its death warrant; hunters wait for hounds to nose the rabbit back, and then they shoot it. If the rabbit would just keep going and going into the next county, it would live to run another day. Why does the rabbit return? It returns for the same reason at Thanksgiving and Christmas and other holidays, highways, trains, and airlines are crowded with people longing to get home again even for just a few hours. Home to rabbit is no different from home to man. Familiar surroundings are comfort, and strange surroundings are stress to all flesh as well to all plants.

All winter I had a geranium in a window with a southern exposure in an upstairs bedroom. With a little water and attention it bloomed the winter long. When frost was no longer a danger, I brought it down and put it on a flower stand on the front porch that is on the north side of the house and where only morning sun gets to it. The geranium stopped blooming, and it stopped growing. Aside from remaining green, one would have guessed that it was dying.

I passed the plant many times a day as I came and went and took notice of its struggle adjusting to its new environment. At first for many days it did nothing that was noticeable. Then, there was a measurable heliotropic movement as all the leaves began to turn toward the direction of the morning sun. Next, buds appeared, and then a bud stem quickly elongated, and the buds opened into blossoms. The trauma of change from one environment to another had been endured and overcome.

I empathized with the geranium's trauma. In my youth I was moved, so to speak, from the bedroom window with a southern exposure to a porch with a northern exposure many times, and I was so preoccupied with adjusting to my new environments I had remaining little psychic energy or exploratory inclination to give to the creation of bloom. Much of my youth was spent in the room of myself where I was no stranger and in which I conjured up pleasant dreams and hopes for future years. I became introverted and learned to live with myself. However, unless one wants to become a monk in a no-speak monastery, he must work his way into the world outside himself.

When I think of moving the geranium, I also think of changing schools. When I was in the fifth grade, my parents moved from the west end of town to the east end. That move alone was traumatic and challenging particularly outside the confines of the new house. As September approached and I had to face the prospect of attending a new elementary school, fear and worry became leeches on my being. When the day came to go to the new school, I was in a state of terror. I retreated into myself just as a terrapin does when danger approaches, and I stayed there for weeks. I was incapacitated with respect to learning. My focus was on adjusting to all the new personalities, their peculiarities, and the halls and walls of the strange environment.

I garden and have since my youth with breaks for war and education. I have been forced on occasions to protect transplants such as tomatoes and cabbages from birds' depredation, particularly starlings. I devised a way to frustrate them: I saved half-gallon, paper milk cartons, and I opened the tops and the bottoms to fashion hothouses of paper for the new plants. When I put a transplanted tomato or other plant in the ground, I slipped a carton over it and secured the carton by shoring up earth around it, thus affording the plant a transitional environment that temporarily protected it from the birds and from the harshness of spring's less benign weather. I discovered the carton not only protected the plant from starlings and other predators, it also served wonderfully as a hot house in which the plant thrived and eventually grew out the top of the carton.

In addition to the trauma of moving many times, I was immersed in what is called today a dysfunctional family. After a number of years of pulling in different directions, my parents separated and divorced in the depths of the Depression. Thus, I had to cope with the challenge of many foreign faces and events, too many for me to consider realistic hopes and the implementation of them. So I dreamed and flowed with the stream.

My savior was the opportunity to live with my grandparents on their farm in the summers and during some winters. There, I found function and structure and a compatible, familiar, and inspiring environment. There, I came to know some of my potential, and I developed some self-respect and gained ballast as well as sail.

But I bloomed late. I spent so much time in my youth holed, up fearing and dreaming, I graduated from high school ranked near the bottom. But after the war, I entered a first rate university and graduated at the top of my class. The difference was in high school I spent most of my energies acclimatizing and integrating internally, preparing as it were ground for growth, while at the university I was able to flower from that intellectual and psychological earth.

Now, when I pass the geranium on the porch and see it in bloom, I say to myself it and I have much in common. All protoplasm, it seems, is as one, and the geranium's life and mine have experienced times that have driven us into ourselves and times that have conduced us to bloom.

Further, it is apparent a child needs to have roots, to have a place with which he is familiar and in which he has a base of security from which he can concentrate on cultivating his potential. Too much change to the strange of places and people and too little compatibility of environment can inhibit a child's blooming just as transplantation can a geranium's.

3

GOING HOME, MAYBE

In August, 1945, I was stationed at Maison
Blanche on an airfield near Algiers when the news
came that a super bomb had been dropped on a
Japanese city and capitulation by the Japanese was
imminent. The war in Europe was over. The Nazis
had been defeated. The prospect now for me was
going home after nearly four years of homesick-
ness, privations, and uncertainty.

On September 3rd it was announced Japan had
surrendered. A weapons carrier arrived with a case
of champagne for my little outfit. It was a joyous
and inebriated day. The war was over, and home
was a real prospect. If I could get from such a far
away place as Algiers back to the hills of West
Virginia, I told myself often, I would never leave
the hills again.

On a day in November about Thanksgiving
time, I received orders out of the blue to be packed
and ready to board an aircraft to be flown to Bone,
Algeria, and there board a ship for the states. I was

advised I could take with me only two barracks bags of personal items; whatever else would have to be abandoned. I had a footlocker I had built of scrap lumber filled with mementoes, and I had just received my Christmas gifts from the states, but I left them. Going home was a high priority, higher than any priority I had ever had.

At the appointed hour I arrived at the airfield burdened with two barracks bags stuffed to overflowing. I boarded the plane and took a seat and waited for the takeoff. Soon, the rather ancient aircraft awoke, and it groaned, sputtered, coughed, whined, and finally caught fire and roared. Now, it was on its way to Biskra, an airfield in the Sahara Desert, at which I had been stationed for nine months. There it picked up a few more soldiers headed home. With them and me, it took off for Bone, Algeria, on the coast of the Mediterranean near Tunisia.

Six other soldiers and I spent the night there, and the next morning we boarded a transport ship that during the war had a contingent of U.S. sailors to man the ship's guns. But they had gone home, and their quarters were free for us. I was no sooner on the ship then the captain requested my presence. He had a radio problem, which I repaired according to him, in miraculous time. He gave me two bottles of Spanish cognac.

So, we sailed the Mediterranean from Bone to the Strait of Gibraltar. What a glorious sail it was! Even in November the air was temperate, the sea and sky were blue, the sun a pot of gold, and the porpoises played the ballerinas day and night just fore of the ship on the port and starboard sides. Then, we sailed through the Strait of Gibraltar, noting Morocco on the port and the British enclave of Gibraltar on the starboard while we entered the vast and unpredictable Atlantic Ocean.

Because it was December, the captain took the southern route; the weather was warm, serene, and romantic, particularly at night. The aft deck where I spent most of the nights was idyllic. The sky and the moon were naked to the eye. The wake trailed white water into infinity, and placidity reigned with nothing but ocean, stars, and moon, the silence broken only by the ship's parting of the waters of the ocean.

We lived high on the hog. This was a transport ship with a crew of civilians, all of whom were well paid and well provided for. The meals were first rate, and the drinks were plentiful. Steaks and potatoes and all else were on the table nightly. Paradise had come to earth.

But the good times soon ended. After nearly

two weeks of sailing in the Mediterranean and the Atlantic in serene waters and just a few days short of docking in Baltimore harbor, a monstrous storm erupted and began to toss the ship like it was nature's play thing. The waves were mountainous. The ship would climb to the crest of one and shake violently because the ship's screw was free of the ocean. Then it would tip into the pit at the foot of the next crest. It would begin the climb to the next crest and shake and then dive into the next pit. And so it went all night long. The dining room had racks on the walls to store condiments such as steak sauce and catsup because on the table they would slide with the sway of the ship. The condiments did not stay in place long, for the ship tipped so far off the perpendicular the bottles of condiments flew out of the rack and banged against the bulkhead. I spent the night in my bunk sliding to the foot of it and then sliding to the head of it, back and forth until dawn. It was reported the next day that a ship north of us had broken apart.

When we entered Baltimore harbor, the cause of the storm was obvious: it was zero cold, but we were almost home, and I was excited. However, we waited and waited to debark the ship, and no order came to do so. Finally, we learned the ship had been quarantined for some reason. But somewhere some officer yelled to some inferior to get those men off the ship pronto, quarantine or no quarantine. He knew what torture it was for soldiers to be so close to home and to be stymied by some bureaucratic detail.

We were ordered to leave the ship by rope ladder over the side in zero weather. I remember looking over the side at the boat bobbing a mile down waiting for me to descend the rope ladder. I said to myself, "If I can get to that boat safely, I am home." So I started the climb down a rag. It took ages to reach that bobbing boat, but I got there, and soon I was on shore.

After being processed at Fort George E. Meade, I left with $300.00, an honorable discharge, and the GI Bill, I contacted an uncle who lived in Baltimore and stayed with him for the night, and the next day he took me to the C&O station where I boarded probably the Fast Flying Virginian for Charleston. When the train stopped at Clifton Forge to my utter and joyous surprise, my mother, unaware I was on it, boarded it. I was really home at last. And I have never left the hills.

4

A JOINT VENTURE WITH NATURE

A few weeks ago the ground was hard from freeze. But yesterday, thanks to a few days of southern winds, I was able to plow the ground and plant those seeds that can endure, without mortal injury, the cold and frost that are to come. I have onion-sets, lettuce seeds, spinach, peas, and beets dropped and covered. I am now in March in a joint venture with nature. I will plow, hoe, weed, and fight against the pests and hope nature will provide the sun and rain. Together, we can produce that without which nothing can survive---food.

I feel better now when it rains and when the sun's warmth stirs life in the earth. I am now a member of that Eternal Partnership, existing from Eden to Doomsday, consisting of nature and farmers dedicated to do what is so fundamental. Without these agrarian members even Wall Street aficionados would have to abandon computer stalls and take to gardening or, more likely, to the preemptive sacking of others' granaries and fruit houses.

No occupation or industry or any entrepreneurial undertaking matters more to humankind than the man with hoe. It's he who produces onions and lettuces and all else that come to table. I become one in spirit with those who toil for little to produce the necessities for those who have much. So it has been and probably always will be. Globalization hasn't changed the timeless inequities suffered by farmers in their trade with cities. Peasants everywhere still lose in the exchange.

But the toilers for little reap the rewards of working hand in hand with nature, whose rewards, however so little, are basic and bring to them not just a wage but also good appetite, sound sleep, and the spiritual comfort the toil they do and income they earn are honest in the sense for every penny earned, they have expended a penny's worth of effort to produce essentials. Few in any other occupation can have the comfort of knowing the wage they receive is commensurate with the value of the labor they do, an exchange whose fairness appalls profiteers whose expectations scorn the concept of equity.

Seeds are miracles. I have read that seeds buried with Pharaohs centuries ago when exposed to water and warmth germinated. They had lain thousands of years in suspended animation and were resurrected when mothered by earth, rain, and sun. And within those seeds and all other seeds is the history of all their antecedents reaching back to First Life, a reach of millions of years. Also, within seeds are not only their history but also their future. If their environment is optimal, they will follow the mandates of their genes, mature, propagate, and produce a new generation of seeds carrying with them all their history plus the pages their parents added. Such is a synopsis of all seeds and all life.

But nature is a capricious partner. It will make a lake of a field one season and a desert of it the next---unmoved by wishes, hopes, and prayers of those who depend on the field for their livelihood. It will whimsically send hail so large and fierce it strips foliage from trees and batters everything in field and garden to tatters, leaving a wasteland where expectation resided. However, there are times when its youthful exuberance and excesses cease and a more mature mother rules. Rain comes gently and then opens the door for the sun to come in. And after a polite period, the rain returns, and then the sun comes again. This fruitful succession is the godsend and benediction the man with the hoe hopes for.

Nature is beyond bribery and partisanship.
When rain comes, it moistens the fields of the
landlord and the tenant. When drought comes,
knight and serf suffer alike. When the earth
quakes, castles and huts come to ruins. Winds
lift the roofs and topple the temples regardless of
status or rank or class. Victors grow complacent
and fat, and the vanquished return to conquer the
conquerors. In nature, nothing fails like success.
Often the meek inherit the earth.

Nature is the consummate artist. Man's art
imitates her. The novelist and playwright depict
human life and its relationships with others and
nature. Poets distill nature to its barest truths
and purest beauties. Artists paint landscapes and
natural scenes and portraits. Musicians organize
and compose the sounds of winds, brooks, birds,
storms, and all the others melodies and cacopho-
nies whispered and wailed on lands and seas and
in the heavens.

And nature is the source of love, loyalty, and
duty. The birds and bees awake at dawn and work
till dusk to build nests and hives, to lay eggs, to in-
cubate their progeny, and wing here and there day
after day providing for their offspring and protect-
ing them against predators. A partridge with chicks
will at her peril attempt to lure away a predator by

faking a broken wing. And divorce is not an option for the robin or the honeybee.

Any entity that can create a seed no larger than a gnat's wing and can grow into leaves of lettuce and then bolt into a stalk that flowers and seeds is a miracle worker. And any entity that is a miracle worker and is evenhanded, honest, open, non-partisan, and is not susceptible to sentimentality, favors, rituals, icons, oratory, supplication, bribery, or politics is the kind of partner one should chose for any venture. And the glory is anyone can choose her without bureaucratic approval or any other ceremony or license and have her as partner for life. But as she is, one must accept her and work to be one with her in spite of her eccentricities, caprices, whimsies, and all her other traits, good and bad, in order to have one's hoped for harvest. Such are the demands of any partnership and marriage.

5

GARDENING FROM WINTER TO SUMMER

I plant onions, lettuce and peas in winter. It's
near the end of that season, but nevertheless by the
calendar, it's winter. I also plant potatoes, beets,
parsley and a few other hardy plants before the
Vernal Equinox. Also, it's not unusual for me to
pick kale and pull turnips in January, the remnants
of the previous August's planting. Gardening is my
fun and therapy and my antidote to idleness---the
Devil's workshop---nearly year around. I suspect
I would have long since been food for worms had
I not gardened, eaten products of the garden, and
worked with plough and hoe under the seasons'
skies.

Little did I imagine as a kid on the farm hoeing
a hilltop of rocky acres under a blowtorch sun in
July one day I would take to gardening with fond-
ness and have bottomland. My grandfather, who
used to smile knowingly at the number of times I
asked him the time of day, (I was praying for noon,
dinner, and an hour's respite.) would be proud of

me now. He may not know it, but he taught me how to work and endure ten hours of sweat labor, an endurance considered torture by today's standard.

I plant onions with confidence, and I always plant twice what I need because onions are easy to plant and certain to grow and immune to frost and freeze. No worm or bug attacks them, and a deer must be starving to death to eat them. Even if a hard rain crusts the ground, the onions poke through. When they are mature, the plant top obliging falls to the ground signaling the end of growth and the readiness to be pulled and stored. No soup or pot roast is fit to eat without the onion. The onion is the first-born and prince of the patch.

Even though frost can burn a potato top to ground level, I plant potatoes in winter because, if frost doesn't come, they are so fully grown by the time the potato beetles surface and begin their mating and egg laying, they survive with a little help the onslaught of the beetles' voracious offspring. And if frost does come, the potato plants revive and continue to grow new leaf. And now since the beetles and their larva are immune to insecticides, I have an environmentally safe system of dealing with them. I take a five-gallon bucket and a hand spade and walk the rows knocking the pests into the bucket with the spade. Then, even while cognizant all life has a place in the Grand Scheme, I, in somber mood adulterated with Darwinism, execute the pest under heal of shoe. Some larva grow fat, but most die under heal, and the potatoes thrive.

Peas, as much mate to potatoes as is bread to butter, could be planted in the fall, and they would survive the rigors of winter and peep through in February, so I plant them in the month of Groundhog Day. Come frost or freeze they grow and bloom and produce an ovary that is seldom less than four or six peas in a pod. Blooms that produce only one of their kind must envy the pea, and capitalists must dream of an investment of one that returns hundreds. But had I had the hammer and anvil upon which the world and all else was created and fashioned, I would have designed the pea as He did the strawberry: when the pea was ready for picking, the pod would turn red or if not red then elderberry blue so one did not have to search for a green pea pod in a sea of green. For one whose age has dimmed his vision, picking peas is tedious as always it has been, but more so when green pods blend with green vines.

Lettuce is a sure thing, a remarkable thing. From a seed, on which a flea couldn't find standing room, comes forth in the cold and rain of late

winter a crisp, delicate, crinkly sheet of green.
Simpson leaf lettuce and I have known one another
time out of mind. A spring ritual in my earliest
memories was wilted lettuce, a combination of leaf
lettuce and spring onions or scallions drenched in
a hot dressing of a chef's balance of bacon grease,
sugar, and vinegar. Lettuce came earlier than sas-
safras tea and poke greens but later than rhubarb
and asparagus, those earliest harbingers of winter's
end.

An entrepreneur who dreams of ten-fold or
twenty-fold increase of investment in a year should
consider strawberries, but not seriously until he
could employ someone who agrees to hours of
stoop and squat labor for little. Twenty strawberry
plants in ground in May will by the next May in
the best of conditions become ten times the number planted, and each member will bud, bloom,
and bear a handful of berries whose shape, color,
texture, and sweetness induced a Caesar to decree
that when ripe they appear on his table, troubling
someone to transport them from sequestered plots
in his empire. That the berries turn red is an esthetic consideration to emperors, but for those
who pick the red berries and know the frustration
of picking green peas amid greenery, they agree
if they must pick, then to pick red among green is

easier than to pick green in green.

I have had on table since late winter and summer's approach asparagus, rhubarb, lettuce and onions, potatoes and peas, broccoli, spinach, beets, kohlrabi, collards, cucumbers, and I have coming in full growth sweet corn in tassel, tomatoes, squash, okra, beans, peppers, garlic, cabbages, Brussels sprouts, and whatever I have overlooked.

My garden is to me my progeny, my dream, my companion, my work, and my daily bread. And it is my hair shirt. I will my body to do the squatting, bending, and sweating to comply with nature's mandate: before rest, there must be work. And even though I do not have to adhere to nature's bidding and could couch the day away, I know in my soul's deepest depths compliance with nature's demand is man's true salvation. Thus is my commitment to knowing nature, learning her lessons, extolling her virtues, marveling her miracles, conserving her riches, and endeavoring to live with the principles she has inscribed in my mind.

6

A MARCH WALK

This March Sunday was a day a poet would have to contemplate long before attempting to reduce its beauty to words. It was a day mostly sunny rather than party cloudy, and the sun when out was a warm embrace and a bright cheer. The eclipsing clouds were soaring dramas scudding herd-like over an earth greened with grass and dappled with the yellow of daffodils. To have been housebound or streetbound or citybound on such a day would have been torture.

March sun is bright, and its brightness is unobstructed. Thus, it pours through every opening and floods everything outdoors with hope and promise of life. Jesus may or may not have entered Jerusalem on a donkey, had his last supper, suffered crucifixion, and arose from His grave during the week after the Vernal Equinox, but the church fathers knew the hope of spring, and they set a fitting and opportune date to remember the Passion and Resurrection. Spirit and body rejoice in the generous light of the Equinox after the sun's stingy months following the Winter Solstice.

While the morning sun lighted my upper room, I seeded pots with sweet and hot peppers, eggplants, and tomatoes and set them in the sun of a bay window in company with a growing cabbage family and other plants already greening and reaching for the sun. The miracle residing within these dry specks, when planted and tended and watched to season's end, is one not even a skeptic can doubt.

The gardens have been plowed and turned. Their under soil is now their topsoil. It looks like chocolate waves of a choppy sea. Plowed ground under a March sun with daffodils in abundance along the side of an abandoned road is beauty and security. Today, except for those gardens of certain counterculture societies and a few hippies, gardens are plowed by tractors, but I remember as a boy plowing a field with a turning plow pulled by a team of horses and viewing the turned acres at the end of day with the incomparable satisfaction that comes from doing a day's work on the land under a March sun and in view of the virgin bloom of the service trees. And, I can relate to Robert Burn's concern at turning up a wee mouse and her household and her best plans gone awry.

The overflow pipe at the pond is busy with a

stream. The ponds, aquifers, and reservoirs are full of rain and the snow of yesterdays. The deed to my land describes the acreage as being at the headwaters of Bradshaw Run. I had a look at Bradshaw's pristine headwaters this March day and found them purling their way down the deep hollow toward Indian Creek, to the New River, thence to the Kanawha, Ohio, Mississippi, and into the Gulf of Mexico. A view of the runoff of spring water down uncluttered streams along hollows populated with trees that have known a century of springs is an arresting scene, a scene that one's genetic ghost longs to blend into.

The cows and calves hug the side of the hill exposed to the south and the returning sun. They seem content to lie and ruminate and enjoy the warmth of the sun and the gnat-free days while waiting for hay time. A new calf with white feet and face sniffs at a salt block exploring the new world it has come into.

The forest floor and mossy rocks without the summer shade are exposed to the glare of March light broken only by the bare trees' shadows. Light invades places not noticed except on such a day, and for that reason, one notes them with the same interest aroused by a view from the dark into a lighted room. The hollow where the Bradshaw

runs is in summer a jungle of undergrowth, but
now with growth in abatement, life in hibernation,
and the place lit with the shine of solar wattage, it
is inviting and accessible.

I walk to places on such a day that I do not walk
to at any other time of the year. With enough coolness to incite movement, warmth to insure comfort, solitude to relax the body and mind, and the
absence of bugs and bees and most other critters,
I walk the hollow and go to see an ancient oak
that once stood alone in a worn pasture. Now it is
a burly gorilla of a tree in a patch of skinny pines
planted as erosion control thirty years ago. The oak
has watched the history here for 300 years. In the
presence of this gnarled ancient, I feel reverence,
the kind of reverence one feels for anything that
has endured seasons for centuries.

Horizons, like train whistles in the night, are romantic. Everything at a distance and in the future
seems to attract and lift the spirit. If man did not
know the past or had no hope of the future or could
see only within reach, nostalgia and lure would die
and romance with them. Being on a high hill on
such a day with a compass view of the countryside
is to be higher than the hill on which one stands.
The spirit on such an occasion stretches beyond
being.

I have been in places with no access to woods and headwaters or horizons when a March day fulfilled the hints of February and predicted the glory of April, and I have known longing and felt loss watching its passing while walking crowded pavements gray. Fate has given me nothing better nor anything more prized than the chance to consummate such a day with a walk in solitude under a March sun amid all the manifestations of earth's resurrections.

7

WINTER'S DEMISE & SPRING'S REPRISE

The first day of this April was coined by the collective daydreams of folks living north of the Tropic of Cancer, their day-shaping reveries conceived during the pinching days when they huddled indoors and winter ruled outdoors. April Fool's day is a day when the sun wins against the wind and when the sun is a sustained caress, an equinoctial day that causes cattle to ruminate on the south side of meadows and man to bask. Even though this day may be short, he knows after spring comes summer. It was a day when one could write it down that winter is gone and spring has arrived.

The meadows are as green as Ireland with a green unique to spring. It is the green of youth, of the first growth following the long hibernation in wait for the sun's return from its sojourn in Capricorn country. When one has in view simultaneously a meadow in spring's green growth and a bush of forsythia in bursting yellow, he sees an arresting contrast and a chorus of color, and he thinks thanks. If one adds to that the colors of the view of a herd of Hereford and Angus cattle grazing on the green with their calves dotted about under the benign sun, he has a scene of spring in which all its glories are in epitome.

The barn loft is empty. It has the look of a bank vault after Dillinger's gang had raided the place. All of last spring's grass that was cut, windrowed, baled, and stored is gone, fed out during winter's drizzle, snow, and freeze to those cattle now with heads down grazing the new growth with their calves lying about with eyes on swollen udders. Abraham, Jehovah's favorite, millennia ago counted in spring his stock and the dividends from it, and Christ spoke of barns, meadows, and lilies of the field. Making inventory of barns, counting cattle and their issue, and looking at the beauty of flowers in the fields were spring time activities of man long before the records in the Good Book were written. And the happy activities are still stored in man's genetic memory holding in awe his spiritual attention as does his viewing the heavens, the hills, the shores, and the seas.

It's daffodil time, the time of those perennials that bring so much joy for so little trouble. I have planted daffodils and replanted daffodils for forty years. I have daffodils everywhere I can plant them. They are like cattle; every year they produce dividends by doubling. The problem is by doing so over time they crowd so tightly, and none have the room they need. One must dig them up and replant them, but for me to keep up with the digging up and replanting, my schedule would be taxed even more than it is. So I enjoy those hardy ones that persist in blooming, the Mt. Hoods, Pheasant Eyes, King Alfreds, and all the other varieties. I pick them and vase them and say to my children look at these closely and consider the challenge to one who has the raw materials and the mandate to create them from scratch. Therein is my religion. The texture, proportion, color, scent, and the sculptured beauty of each flower that arises from an onion-like bulb every spring without fail if given room is a wonder and a mystery that eclipses man's best efforts to out-god God.

Water, indispensable to existence, is more abundant in spring than at any other time except at times of nature's rampages. The streams swell in pregnancy with waters green and pure from the antisepsis of winter's cleansing chill. My farm, reads the records, lies at the headwaters of Bradshaw Run, Forest Hill District, Summers County, WV, USA. Bradshaw Run on my place even in flood stage can be crossed by an easy jump. But it flows into Indian Creek that empties into the New River, which in confluence with the Greenbrier, cascades down the gorge from Hinton to Gauley Bridge where the Gauley with them form the Kanawha. The waters of the Kanawha move leisurely after all the rush into the Ohio, then on to Cairo, Illinois, and from there the waters from Bradshaw Run and all its acquaintances meander Mississippi's channel to the Gulf of Mexico, where the sun and southwest winds in concert bring those waters back to the meadows from where they flowed in the beginning. All is a circle, a reprise.

My garden is plowed and planted. I have peas and potatoes up, lettuce and onions shootings, asparagus thumb-thick and as high, spinach and beets peeping through, and rhubarb ready for first harvest. The apple trees are in full bud, the cherry in bloom, and the pear at the cherry's heel. And I have tomatoes seeded growing in the sun of the south windows and leaning into the sun like children enthralled by some rare happening outdoors.

Sidewalk philosophers often observe what goes around comes around. They have in mind outrageous conduct is often repaid with outrageous conduct. Pride goes before a fall. But there is more to the saw than they think. For one needs only to look at the face of a clock to understand man's life is a circle. Around and around he goes: seconds, minutes, hours, days, months, years; dawn, noon, twilight, and dark. But the seasons are the merry-go-round that is a delight and a marvelous drama of which spring's reprise is the story of resurrection and renewal.

8

An Earthday of Equinoctial Enjoyment

April 3rd dawned with the full moon appearing like a perfect pearl atop the ridge of a hump mountain. It was the first full moon after the equinox and thus the prelude to Good Friday and Easter. The weather was warm, and the sky was starlit, all of which predicted a day to enjoy and remember.

My day was in the hands of fate, for I had no plans except what she decided. When I went to the post office, she stepped in and decided the matter: I was delivered a box in which were twenty-four strawberry and ten asparagus plants. By now the sun was up, and the world was warm and bright. The sky had the blue of infinity but veiled with gossamer. With nothing else pressing, I made plans to go to the farm and plant the plants knowing the earlier they were in the ground, the better chance they had to survive.

At the farm I entered spring's haven. The meadows were Irish green and lush from the recent rains. The herd of blacks, browns, and whitefaces were all grazing in one direction with heads to ground, vastly different from just a few weeks ago when they stood with brute patience, heads up, waiting for a hand out. The mockingbirds at their fence-post residences winged up and settled down making mock music. The barn swallows, Top Guns of the Avian Corps, displayed their unequalled maneuvers. The bluebirds darted in and out of a hole in a dead tree. The phoebes with bobbing tails came and went nest building. And the robins with heads up and breasts out hopped and looked, and listened and hopped again to look and listen some more.

The garden I had earlier plowed twice looked rich and damp. I had covered most of it with horse manure last fall, and the treatment was evident: where I had planted onions, lettuce, spinach, and peas, I found them all up and healthy. The strawberry patch I planted two years ago had resurrected from a freezing winter and had a few blooms in it.

After noting all this, I set to work to do what I had come to do: plant the new strawberry and the asparagus plants. Since I had plowed, fertilized, and laid off in anticipation of the arrival of the strawberry plants, I had now only to hoe hills for twenty-four plants and plant them. I did the hilling and then dropped a plant at each hill and procceded to spade and finger the plants in. It was a sort of tucking them in a bed for the night but in this case for the season. My bones are old, and my musculature out of exercise, so I went about the tucking in with snail deliberation. I would drop to one knee and do the spading from that position. Then I would rise slowly and move to the next hill, drop to one knee, and so on until all were tucked in. Now it is up to nature, my partner in this venture.

With the strawberries set aside, I turned my attention to the asparagus plants. Planting asparagus is a different work from planting strawberries. An asparagus patch properly planted and cultivated will continue after a year or so to produce tablesize asparagus for years.

So, first I bring the heavy tiller to the patch and plow deeply. Then I bring the smaller tiller with a furrow blade attached and plow a deep furrow. Having already with shovel and bucket scrounged around the pasture collecting cow piles, I distribute the manure in the ditch; then with a posthole digger I dig ten holes. I pour rainwater in each hole and then drop an asparagus plant in each. Finally, I spade and tuck the plants in and cover the whole with loose soil. This year, if all goes well, the plants will be thin and willowy but not large enough to eat. When they mature and a plant comes up and is cut for the table, a message goes down to send another up to receive the life-giving light of the sun. And up one comes.

By now the weather is so warm I remove my shirt. The equinoctial sun is benign and feels therapeutic on my bare torso, and the winds from the south caress instead of push. I look up from the work and note a cherry tree in its full wedding-day glory and think of A. E. Housman's poem "Loveliest of Trees, the Cherry Now." Enthralled with the beauty of the tree at Eastertide, Housman counts the years he has remaining to view it. He takes twenty, his age, from seventy, the Biblical allotment, and writes: "And since to look at things in bloom / Fifty springs are little room, / About the woodlands I will go / To see the cherry hung with snow."

Housman lived to be 77, so he had 57 years of room to go about the woodlands and see the cherry trees in Easter dress. At 86, my years left of seeing my cherry tree in wedding attire are few. But I have had nine more than Housman, and for that I am grateful.

After the work I sat on the porch of the 100-year-old farmhouse and viewed all of spring's wonders and beauties. None of the noise, rush, madness, or trash of modern life spoiled the quiet and sights. The world was its greenest green on land, and the forests had that altered look. The birds were busy, and the bees vied with them for the title of the busier. The cherry tree was alive with bees and other insects seeking the sweets of blooms. The whole of the world was in a wedding, a wedding that would serve to propagate it with a new generation of every living thing. As I sat there, I had the wish for more room, like say, fifty years more.

Thus ended the gift of the equinox, a day spent in grass-root activities amid a confluence and conjunction of weather and place one would pray for, doing that which is basic to life: seeding the soil with plants designed to provide food for the planter.

9

The Drama of a Spring Day

I awoke at five thirty to a darkened dawn. Once uncovered, I knew the temperature was mild and noted hints that winter's chill had been swept out of the house. Outdoors winter was retreating to the northland. From the window I could see it driven by an army of menacing black-bottomed clouds, attended beneath with gusts and grey swirling fog. The growling mass was punctuated periodically with breaks in the grey through which poured from an azure patch eye-squinting and radiant sunshine into an atmosphere cleansed by the night's showers.

To observe the drama, I walked clothed in a light jacket. The air was damp, but the temperature optimum, so long as the clouds covered the sun. But when the break came, in a lightening suddenness, the sun starred on infinity's stage. Then, the jacket was too much, and so the alternation from cool to warm continued during the entire walk. A moment too cool then a moment too warm is the epitome of the nature of spring.

I walked the river bridge, a span near a quarter of a mile. The river was clear and filled with spring rain and thundershowers. It has flowed perpetually and followed eternally a course laid out eons before humans inhabited the earth. A creek enraged with too much rain entered the vast river in a tantrum and in a frenzy of haste to empty itself. The confrontation between Madam's Creek and New River conjured the image of a child beset with frustration beating the knees of a parent. The river's indifference to the tantrum reflected its geological priority and relentless resolution in search of a sea.

All the while the tree swallows were out in force maneuvering maniacally over the roiling river feeding on a mysterious and non-visible sustenance emanating from the water.

The mountains have reigned around the town the winter long as mortuaries of barren boles: no sign of life. But now there is a perceptible alteration. A pink glow envelops them, and here and there an upstart exhibits a glimmer of chartreuse, which is upstaged by the earliest white of the service tree. In the town the dogwoods are having their day displaying splendid trees of flowering pinks, inducing the image of a gaggle of girls garlanded for gaiety.

I have known since its youth a golden delicious apple tree and have enjoyed its fruits. It has been

blooming and blooming for days, and today buffeted
by winds, under the clouds and in the sunshine, it is
a marvel to behold. I cannot contain myself from
sharing the wonder of this tree. It is a miracle of
blooms. It is as though it had heard of the hard times
and decided to do its best to provide for the world's
poor an apple a day. In addition it brighten the world
with a gargantuan bouquet of rose-colored petals,
a bouquet alive with bees. Soon, the wedding will
end, and the tree will have to doff the dress and don
the apron, such is the reality of conjugal unions.

The dandelions have appeared overnight and covered a yard like paratroopers dropped from above,
but they are armed only with yellow and have no
goal but to stay put, feed the bees, and seed the soil
around them. Violets, the demure corps of yellow-
eyes draped in lavender, welcome them.

The queen of purple is the lilac. She reigns in
lawns, on yards, and wherever the lord of the land
decides to place her strategically to turn the heads
of spring lovers with her velvet gown. However, she
must compete with the peasants of purple, the red-
bud, along miles of decorated highway valleys.

The grass is green and lush sporting the teen-green
look of health, vigor, and vitality. It's a resurrection
from the barren brown of the drought years. Grass is
as immortal as the gods and will grace spring when

religions are history, because without grass, an earth of dirt would be intolerable to men and gods.

The drama of spring involves intrinsically the competition between the wind and the sun. The wind bets the sun wanderer yonder wearing a jacket will keep the jacket on by chill of her wind, and the sun bets the wind wanderer yonder will shed his jacket from the heat of his sun. So on an April day like today, the contest begins. Early the wind wins, and by noon there is no contest; the wind has it. Then the sun comes out and heats everything everywhere, and the rover sheds his jacket.

Today, winter and summer danced the flamenco in the streets, in the treetops, along mountain ridges, and everywhere. At times winter danced it, and at times summer danced it. It was like being in no-man's land between the trenches of warring weathers. But in the end---after both were exhausted from trying to maintain their sovereignty---the season of light had prevailed. But night was coming, and one knows not what casualties will litter the lawn at dawn from such cosmic combat.

The wind of winter was tested and bested by the sun of summer. It will always be so in April unless nature is so contorted by the desecrations and expediencies of humans the very seasons will not know when to come and leave or how to be when here.

10

A Day to Live For & Die After

There have been a number of days in my life at the end of which I have told myself: "I can die now and miss nothing because I have experienced on this day all life's joys, all those joys one can wake to remember with harmonic pleasure and without a tinge of doubt, regret, or remorse."

The setting and constituents of those days have been essentially the same, and the only obstacle to rapture has been the knowledge most humans joy not and will not as I have.

A day in May was such a day. It was a day in which summer was cocooned in early spring, but metamorphosis seemed imminent: haze and broken clouds inhibited the sun's effects except for moments when its warmth induced skin prickles and raised hopes. It was a dry day after many days of spring rain and damp air, perfect weather for meadows, peas, potatoes, lettuce, cabbage, asparagus, and rhubarb. The trees were in full leaf, lavender irises bloomed, and the peach tree of four springs bore a dozen marble-size fruits.

I had escaped in early afternoon the world of telephones, desks, judgments, and titles to go to the land of my ancestors; I called it Celia's Place. I have there an antique house; a garden with nine bean rows, more or less; cows and a bull and their progeny; calves lying languidly on north-side slopes; acres of spring-grass; black walnut trees, locusts, ancient oaks, cherry, peach, apple, and pear; and frog-inhabited ponds.

I plowed with a Troy-Bilt, a rein-less horse, heeding neither gee or haw and a luxury my grandfather, who rose from ox power to horse power in a lifetime, would have marveled at but would have scorned for its seductive power to lead one from the strait and narrow, a way grown weedy since his day.

I plowed earth onto which I have hauled and spread hundreds of bags of leaves, twenty years of composted garbage and lawn cuttings, and bales and bales of straw, and I noticed with satisfaction the friable and rich texture of earth once clods and clay. The smooth, steady glide of the plow chewed its way through the loose, fecund, rock-free soil, a soil condition foreign to my grandfather whose land covered thinly an avalanche of cliffs.

Robins warily followed the tilling, pecking the

exposed earthworms and grubs whose domiciles had been violated like Burn's wee mouse. A killdeer, an exquisite, jewel-like phantom, in punctuated runs on legs of illusions reconnoitered, and the stealth-bomber of the barnyard, the swallow, maneuvered with grace and agility at below radar scope pursuing in full throttle the unseen.

I hoed, a practice from the Stone Age designed to save the cultivated from the uncultivated, recently planted strawberries and pinched off the bloom to direct their sustenance to runner production of offspring for the crop next May. I hoed potatoes and felt the pride of parenthood at the hale and hearty leaf, dark in chlorophyll green.

I picked asparagus, some thumb-thick and some pencil-thin and a two-gallon bucket of crinkled spinach, lettuce, and some romaine, which was at the stage where it looked like a ballet dancer on toes with arms above and hands lilting in languor. I pulled and leafed rhubarb, a weed when combined with applesauce becomes rhuple, a natural with hot biscuits. I gathered green onions, the succulent sizzles of spring.

All these vegetables I washed in buckets of rainwater dipped from the rain barrel sitting under the downspout. To wash vegetables in rainwater is a process to note because it does for the soul what watching wood burn in a fireplace does: it evokes a million years of genetic memories of techniques of living and survival.

I went to the barn to a stall housing a cow and a calf that were not mother and child, to see how the bonding of the cow, who had lost her calf at birth, was progressing with the calf, who had been separated from her mother, a dairy cow whose milk would go to market. The surrogate mother was not taking to the calf and was employing evasive tactics, but the calf was attacking the udder left and right and rear with a vigorous and persistent strategy. I filled a bucket with feed for the cow, and while she stood to eat, the calf sucked and hunched, its tail telling the tale of conquest.

I returned to the pavements gray and remembered the days when I yearned in my heart's core for such a day as this May day and the times when I believed happiness was wherever I was not. I went to the bookcase and found a poem this day had brought to mind. I read it and neared tears from the beauty of it, from the sadness, from the joy of my day, and from the happy thought had William Butler Yeats accompanied me, he would have understood my saying: "I can die now; life has no more to offer."

I will arise and go now, and go to Innisfree,
And a small cabin build there, of clay and wattles made;
Nine bean rows will I have there, a hive for the honey bee,
And live alone in a bee-loud glade.

And I shall have peace there, for peace comes dropping slow,
Dropping from the veils of morning to where the cricket sings;
There midnight's all a glimmer, and the noon a purple glow,
And evening full of the linnet's wings.

I will arise and go now, for always night and day
I hear lake water lapping with low sounds by the shore;
While I stand on the roadway, or on the pavements gray,
I hear it in the deep heart's core.

11

In Praise of Diffusion

I live in a town nestled amid mountains. In this part of the state, the ratio of towns to mountains is one to hundreds, and the ratio in size is miniature to massive. I can walk the bridge over the New River, and no matter in which direction I look, the sight I see is a mountain or mountains, and the only way out of town is down the river or up a creek. This time of the year covered with trees, those mountains are green, the green of spring. There is not a scratch on them except for the cut of a power line here and there and a rare treeless spot for a homestead. And on every limb and twig of those trees are leaves. I often wonder just how many leaves there are within the scope of my sight. To count them would be similar to counting the sands of seashores.

Even more remarkable is every leaf is a photosynthetic factory that uses water from the ground, light from the sun, and carbon dioxide from the air to produce a sugar to sustain the tree and provide energy for its functions. A byproduct of photosynthesis is oxygen, and every leaf releases oxygen into the atmosphere.

When I walk the bridge and look about at all the mountains and at all the trees on those mountains and all the leaves on those trees, which are, in the light of day, doing nothing but producing sugar, exhaling oxygen, and sending it up their smoke-stacks, so to speak, I am astonished, particularly when I consider what I see is just a few acres of what the whole of West Virginia is: essentially an oxygen factory.

While walking and thinking about the amount of oxygen produced by this state, I remembered respiration, the reverse of photosynthesis. Whenever a person breathes, he respires; that is, he absorbs oxygen, consumes sugar, and exhales carbon dioxide. This thought led to calculating the amount of carbon dioxide exhaled by the citizens of a city, say, the size of Charleston and, in addition, the amount of carbon dioxide smoke-stacked into the atmosphere from the city and its environs. Also, I remembered this: coal is dead plant life compressed by tons of earth over a period of millions of years. When coal burns, the carbon dioxide plant life absorbed millions of years ago in the photosynthetic process is released into the atmosphere.

The world now is awash in carbon dioxide. The excess of it appears to have caused climate change, and the change, if it continues, will bring no end of troubles to the peoples of the earth. The solution to the excess of carbon dioxide is trees and more trees to absorb the excess.

Now an oxygen factory in a world starved for oxygen and may be destroyed by carbon dioxide is the savior of the peoples of the world. West Virginia is in fact an oxygen factory. I know it is, for every morning when I walk the bridge, I see all those mountains, all those trees, and all those leaves producing oxygen, and I see few people and few other things that absorb oxygen. This state has an excess of oxygen. Then I wondered why the excess of oxygen here doesn't cause me to hyperventilate and the excess of carbon dioxide in Kanawha Valley cause the people there to suffocate? The answer is a sine qua non, to wit: diffusion. Diffusion is defined by the *Encyclopedia Americana* as "the spontaneous spreading or movement of matter caused by the random motion of molecules. Diffusion occurs down a concentration gradient---that is, the molecules move from a region where they are in high concentration to areas in which their concentration is lower."

If it were not for the phenomenon of diffusion, all the atmosphere around my town would be heavy with oxygen, and the atmosphere in the Valley would be dangerously, if not lethally, heavy with carbon dioxide. But nature anticipated that problem, and she devised diffusion, which causes the heavy concentrations of oxygen in my town to equalize with the lower concentrations of it in the Valley and causes the heavy concentrations of carbon dioxide in the Valley to equalize with the lower concentration of it in my town.

I believe the people of the Valley and the people of the world owe thanks to West Virginia for all the trees it has, all the leaves the trees have, all the oxygen those leaves produce, and all the carbon dioxide those trees absorb.

If oxygen could be treated like land, surveyed off and bought and sold, West Virginians who own forested mountains would be rich, and the urban folks would have to pay dearly to breathe. Of course, the mountain folks would have to buy carbon dioxide to feed the trees, but the excess of carbon dioxide a deadly concentration in the Valley would lower the price of it. That is, market economics would for once favor mountaineers unless some entrepreneur cornered the carbon dioxide supply sky-rocketing the price.

If one were to drop a milligram of iodine in the Atlantic Ocean at Myrtle Beach, theoretically in time the molecules of that milligram would diffuse to the four corners of the Earth. A molecule would show up somewhere on the shores of the Sea of Okhotsk, which washes the seashores of the Kamchatka Peninsula. When I learned this, I began to wonder whether or not good deeds and bad deeds by people diffused; does an act of spiritual love diffuse to all the populations of the world and become an eternal parcel of the Larger Love, an entity which is the sum total of good deeds from time immemorial? Do these acts of love become immortal and forever inspire love, generosity, charity, compassion, and mercy in the hearts of people throughout the world?

In living life one leaves a wake as does a ship, and the wake is the result of his or her good and bad deeds. Do the good deeds live in the memory of the recipients, and then the recipients, by virtue of those memories, do good deeds ad infinitum? If so, then praising diffusion for its miracles with molecules and with people's good deeds is in order.

12

EARLY SUMMER

The days are long filled with light and twilight from dawn to dusk. The sun comes early and leaves late. Noon is a golden queen whose writ runs farthermost now. The night's reign is imperceptibly shortened until the Summer Solstice. Then with little notice, minute by minute, night extends itself until by September it contends equally for sovereignty of the northern heavens.

Summer with it green and warmth is the matured promise of spring, full freedom from the white and ice of winter. One walks with his face to the sky's horizon charmed by the infinite blue spotted with great puffs of soaring cotton clouds and thinks how rare the days really are in June. And this June has had more than its share of rare days.

May was all rain, but rain brings grass, and grass is hay when mowed, baled, and barned. And the sight of a new mown field is arresting and causes one to gaze upon its newly shorn and uniform appearance. Today haymaking is relatively a sweatless task done by tractor and machines that cut the grass and pack it into either bales or rolls. There is no need for a pitchfork, a tool that was as indispensable as a hoe and an ax in my grandfather's day when horses pulled a mowing machine that cut it and a rake that windrowed it for hands that followed with pitchforks to shock it, load it on a wagon, and pitch it into the barn loft. In June at noon under the sun in a hay field, the use of a pitchfork broke sweat from brow and body and gave exceeding value to a dipper of spring water and to the table fare the women prepared.

All the rain has greened the hillsides and meadows with emerald shades not unlike an Irish landscape. The temperatures have been mild, the days warm, and the nights cool. The streams have a look of life and health, not that sickly, septic, emaciated look that comes with drought. The oak in the back and the maple in the front lawn are oases of shade and breeze. And the birds are everywhere.

The phoebes raised two families on one of the porch posts preempting my use of the swing most of the summer. Then after the phoebes had left, a barn swallow dabbed a nest atop what the phoebes had built, and as of yesterday, there were five swallows' heads vying in a frenzy for what mother carried in. The grace, glide, and maneuverability of a barn swallow is a show I never tire watching. A ballerina is an ox in comparison. Through the door glasses I have watched a parent streak across the porch and light like a feather at the edge of the nest, a marvel of aeronautics and aesthetics.

A hummingbird came through an open screen door into a screened-in porch and exhausted itself against the screen and ceiling until it fell to the floor apparently dead. I picked it up and held it in my hand with its underside up. Its wee feet were entangled with spider webs I pulled away. I noticed some life, and after a minute or so, it moved, turned over, and took to the air and away. A jewel of a creature. An incredible creation. I thought while holding it of lines from William Blake: "To see a world in a grain of sand, / And a Heaven in a wild flower, / Hold Infinity in the palm of your hand, / And eternity in an hour. "

I have been introduced to another creature this summer, a creature marvelously adapted and fashioned to prosper. But its prosperity is my garden's poverty. It is a short-tailed shrew, an animal I have had no acquaintance with until this summer. Its occupation of my garden was first noticed when a luxuriant row of pea vines produced no peas. Something, I discovered, had eaten all of them. Then the pulled beets had large cavities hollowed out and the same with the potatoes, the cucumbers, and the half-runners. I began to see the furtive flight under cover of vegetation of a strange critter and found many holes in the rows of everything near the ground. Although the shrew is an another marvel of nature, it does not stand in my estimation equally with the hummingbird. In fact, I am devising ways to rid my garden of shrews, whatever it takes short of destroying the garden in my efforts.

Sitting on the porch fanned by a sweet breeze, I thought of the disparity of my attitude toward the birds and the shrew. Both have a place in nature, and both are miracles of creation, but the former I smile upon, and the latter I frown upon and would dispatch with a hoe if I could aim well enough and were fast enough. I concluded tentatively, always tentatively, that man's ethics and morality encompass and extend only to man and not to any other form of life, nor does it encompass or extend to men of other tribes in times of hostilities with them. Man can bait a barbed hook and lure the unsuspecting to the frying pan. He can set traps and use decoys to kill. He can sit quietly at dawn in a tree stand and assassinate animals doing nothing but having their breakfast. And he can bomb cities destroying infrastructure and killing the young and the aged indiscriminately and then pin medals upon the chests of those who kill with the most efficiency. Man's morality apparently has little to do with the morality of God who created the hummingbird as well of the shrew. Man's moral perspective, save the radicalism of some eccentrics, is basically limited to homo sapiens and   to that species only if it is of the right nationality.

Sitting there with a rare day in June looking all about at the shaded lawn and watching the swallows come and go, I thought of more of nature's manifestations: the movement of the winds, the flow of the waters, the sail of the clouds, the rise and set of the sun and moon, the leap of a deer, the patience of brutes, the green of summer, the yellow of fall, the tears at a grave, the tithe to a cause, and others displays that fill man's days, nights, and seasons.

I put out of my mind the other prescriptions of nature, those unfavorable to man's welfare from his perspective but advantageous to other species, such as fleas, bedbugs, spiders, snakes, crows, and shrews.

Summer is when the living is easy. But its very beginning is the beginning of its end, just as birth is accompanied by death, which tags along until its time. For man and shrew it has been a good summer so far, but I have in mind, I confess, making the remainder of summer not so good for the shrew.

13

NEW YORK WATCHES IOWA CORN GROW

The Associated Press reports a camera focused day and night on an Iowa cornfield since May 17 has captured the attention of thousands of Web watchers who are "fascinated by the sight of the cornstalks getting taller with each passing day and have been e-mailing their appreciation." A teacher in New Jersey uses the CornCam Web to teach her students about farm life. And a publisher in New York says the view of the corn growing is the rage among his co-workers. As cheerleaders they recite encouragement: "Go, Corn! All of New York City is pulling for you."

It is well they do pull for the corn, for without it and all else Iowa and other farm states grow, the Big Apple would starve or have to roam the countryside in armed bands to forage at their peril. I have often wondered how many New York City citizens ever considered how tenuous and precarious is their condition with respect to their food supply and also how only a few inches of topsoil is the difference between living and dying for them and all of humankind.

Whatever they think in that regard, I am happy to learn they have an eye on corn in Iowa and are watching its progress. Further, I am certain I could help the teacher in New Jersey teach her students about farm life in general and corn growing in particular, for I lived a good part of my youth on a farm and learned about corn harvest from seeding to shucking, as well as hay harvest, wheat harvest, oat harvest, and every other kind of harvest. Also, this very day, June 10, 2000, I have seeded four rows of Golden Queen sweet corn, my third seeding this season after a patch of Sun Glow and Silver Queen, a sight which would bring raves from New Yorkers or from anyone who appreciates the miracle of seeds and the taste of corn in all its many forms.

During the winters of the thirties on the wall of the upper porch of my grandfather's farmhouse, I recall seeing seed corn hanging, drying, and waiting for spring, waiting for May. This is the month when oak leaves become the size of a squirrel's ear, an event that signals the time has come to plant the corn.

But before then beginning as early as February, there was much preparation. Always in February would come a drying up and a warm spell, the same one that caused Maple sap to rise. It was then the horses were harnessed, hitched to the sled on which was loaded the turning plow, driven to a far field, and worked to turn the land. Then, the land had to be dragged, harrowed, disked, and laid off in rows.

Planting was often a family affair. Everyone available came to the field to drop fertilizer and three to four seeds to a hill and to cover them with hoes. There was no mechanized planting on the hillside farms in Appalachia in the thirties just as there had not been since the hillbillies had settled in the mountains. It was all oxen at first, and then came horses, plows, and men. Women and girls and boys followed with hoes. In the fall the same crew came with corn cutters and shucking pins except the females were exempt from corn cutting.

After the earth, water, and sun had resurrected the corn seeds from their hibernation and the seedlings had peeked through, the job of the boys and girls was to thin it. Children were closer to the ground, and thus the stooping chore was not so backbreaking as it was for adults. So I went with my grandfather as early as age five to thin the corn to two plants per hill. Even then I felt a discomfort in pulling from the ground the green spirals that had so wonderfully evolved from a shriveled-up, dried-up, apparently lifeless grain to a green, living plant with the potential of producing corn cakes, hominy, and no end of good things.

I learned early to hoe corn. It was a daunting experience. I can remember standing at the beginning of a weedy, ten-acre cornfield with hoe on a hot day in June looking to the end of it and wondering if ever I would reach it. Hoeing corn was a matter of cutting out all the weeds around the corn hill, bending over to pull out the weeds too close to the corn, then hilling up dirt around the plants, clearing the area between the hills, and going to the next one all the while enduring the gnats, the sweat bees, the blazing sun, and the sweat filling the eyebrows. The hours were 6:00 A.M. to noon and from 1:00 P.M. to 6:00 P.M. with a few water-jug breaks or a dip from a spring.

From hoer I graduated to plower. Before age twelve I routinely rounded up the horses and drove them into the barn, harnessed Old Dick, went to the field with the cultivating plow, and plowed. It was tough work. Most of the fields were hillside, and most were rocky. So a job that at best was hard was even harder on steep, rocky land. Further, horses have a mind of their own, and one had to watch, or the horse would destroy more corn than he helped cultivate. It was giddup, gee, haw, and whoa row after row until the chore was done.

At the end of each row, the plow and horse had to be turned and headed into the next row. Usually the cornfield was bordered with woodland, and the horse and I were eager to get to the end to have the relief of a bit of shade and to escape the incessant attack of gnats. The horse and I hurried to the end of a row but slowly began another one. I learned from a horse that horse flesh and human flesh have much in common.

The corn grew, and after the second hoeing and third plowing, it had the upper hand over the weeds, and it was set aside to do the best it could until harvest time. I have lived to see a machine that goes into a corn field, cuts the corn, shucks it, shells it, spits out the fodder, and delivers the grain into a waiting truck. It was not like that in the thirties in Appalachia, not by a long shot. But the field after harvest by machine would never inspire a poet to write about corn in the shock and frost on the pumpkin.

Corn harvest time was in late September during those days when the mornings are cool and foggy and the afternoons are clear and burning hot. My grandad would have me up in the morning before 4:00 and in the field by 5:00. Then, dressed in bib

overalls, long-sleeved shirts, and straw hats and
armed with a corn cutter, an instrument not unlike a machete, we would wade like foot soldiers
of the Crusades into the patch striking with sword
at the ankles of the infidel cornstalks. We would
hold the cut ones until the left arm was full and
then eventually stand the cut corn up tying it into a
shock. Rows of conquered corn decorated the field
at the end of day.

And the day ended unusually early for farm
worker. The heat of afternoon sun in September,
the long sleeves to protect against stinging cater-
pillars, the cutting edge of dried corn leaves, the
gnats and sweat bees, and muscle labor were too
much to bear any longer. So by three or three-
thirty we would call it a day, enjoy a look at the
harvest in neat shocks in military ranks, and turn
for home and supper, that farm meal always fit for
Jupiter and Juno and all the other divines.

In November after October's gold and blue days
had dried the corn, there was a corn shucking usually held at night in the shed of a barn. Families
came, and by lantern light the men and women
threw the corn shocks one at a time to the floor of
the shed, and the shuckers with their shucking pins
pulled back the shucks, broke off the corn, and
tossed the bright yellow ears into a bin where they

lay until used to keep stock and humans alive during winter's barren days.

The neighbors' children came, and while the work progressed, the boys and girls scrambled about in the loft, jumped into hay from one level to another, and in general had a ball as children will when left to their creations. In the light of the lantern, the shadows of shucking and playing danced about the barn's interior and reflected the communal work and merriment of peasants and their labor preparing for Thanksgiving and Christmas and the hunkering down 'til spring.

New Yorkers watching Iowa corn grow are lucky to get to see it if even on a Web page, but they may have missed something elemental: working intimately with nature to produce the essentials of life, enjoying the reward of harvest at season's end, and seeing first hand nature's miracles and beauties. Urban sophisticates often look upon mountain people as hicks and a sub-species, but the man with the hoe will be here long after most all else is extinct. Earth and work are how it all began, and nothing has changed the essential and eternal worth of either.

14

TREES AND BOYS

Every boy has a special spot in the woods. It's a genetic thing: a memory in every cell of every boy of his experiences in the woods since there have been boys. It is a place where trees are a canopy under which a floor of cushiony decayed foliage and moss grow, and all about lichen covers rocks. It is a sequestered spot any calendar would hope to display and a place life seeks in cold of winter and heat of summer. Nearby there is a spring from which a boy can have a draft of clear coolness by moving away leaves, waiting until it's clear, and drinking with cupped hands or face down. But take the trees away, and the spot is nothing to boys or birds or anything.

I knew of a place as a boy. In fact, I knew of many such places, and they were my homes in the woods. But adults often disturb a boy's world. One day men came to look at the woods at one of my favorite spots. My grandfather had agreed to sell on the stump trees for mine posts. He walked the woods and marked with a nick in the bark those that were not to be cut. Unbeknownst to him before the cutting was done, I nicked a few of my special trees and saved them so my woods would not have that naked look and lose the aura of security it provided for me and boys like me.

I remember the chestnut trees and the death of them. What a loss. Nature gave man few gifts greater than the chestnut trees. They provided beauty, nuts by the buckets, fence rails that would last a century, backlogs that sparked in the fireplace, shingles for roofs, and, finally, the easiest to split kindling of any wood.

After the corn was cut and shocked, I have spent fall days getting in the wood to warm by in winter. I would ask my grandfather to spare a certain tree, and I never saw one fall that I didn't feel a certain regret at its passing. If a fallen tree rode down a smaller tree and pinned it, I wasn't comfortable until I had freed the pinned tree so it could reach for the sun again.

I knew trees. I learned from my grandfather the name of every tree that grew in the tree kingdom. I knew a gum when I saw it, an oak and all its kind, a sugar maple, a hickory, poplar, sarvus, dogwood, locust, the various pines, and, of course, the royal chestnut and many more. I knew those that would split easily and those that resisted splitting. I knew their leaves and bark.

In biology, I learned what in my heart I knew must be so: trees exhale oxygen and inhale carbon dioxide, and humans inhale oxygen and exhale carbon dioxide. That is, trees produce what boys must have to breathe and live, and boys produce what trees must have to breathe and live.

Over the years, I watched eroded land become productive again by trees. First, came the locusts and pines to the eroded land. Then after years of growth and foliage waste from those trees, the land became fertile enough to sustain hardwoods. Then, came the oaks and maples. The evolutionary process was repeated and in that enduring hope in this process; nature heals manmade sores.

On land owned by the heirs of pioneers there was a forest that I had driven by for years. It had a majesty about it. The heirs sold it to sub-dividing speculators who first sold the timber, and then in came the bulldozers and chainsaws. Now it has the appearance of those pictures after the battle of Belleau Wood in France during WWI. I avoid looking at it when I pass. It has the effect on me of the view of a corpse.

I read once that lumbermen felled a white oak in Pickaway, Monroe County, which was six feet in diameter at the stump, and from it came 3,000 board feet of lumber and seven cords of wood.

I grieved a bit over this. The thought of such a tree cut seemed a sin. And it seems a sin that, of the thousands of such trees once here, there is scarcely one such tree that has escaped the ax and the saw. Will there come a day when a boy cannot find a spot in the woods he knows in his genes is the place to plan and play?

I venture that juvenile attention disorder and delinquency as well as adult neuroticism, addictions, and criminality would never have reached the proportions they have, had humankind not forsaken nature. People leave suburbs and cities to travel hundreds of miles to jostle with other folk for a place in the woods for a week to rejuvenate their atrophied ties with nature and to give their children just a touch from the Mother of everything, but what they need is an embrace, a close relationship, an understanding, and a spiritual sustenance only she can provide. Poetry helps, but it is no substitute for spring in the woods.

Art is a reflection of nature. How many painting and photographs are there of a stream beginning in a sylvan background, purling through a cathedral of trees, and terminating either in a delta of meadows or a cascade of water into a pristine pool?

Countless---for these scenes are places where men and boys and women and girls through eons gathered and found support for body and soul. Written within us all is the genetic memory of them and the yearning for them.

Man paints a forest scene of magnetic lure and of exquisite colors, and later generations reduce the real scene to wreckage in order to build a museum to house the painting, exhibiting their preference for the painter's creation over those of nature. And so it is with many of humankind's doings. Arrogance seduces people to play God with only an infinitesimal bit of knowledge relative to the omniscience of the Creator. Ignorance breeds hubris. And man's hubristic efforts to improve on nature have denied many boys the companionship and spiritual nurture of trees.

15

THE MIRICALE OF SEEDS TO MEALS

If I were to place one each of the following seeds in the palm of my hand, the space covered would be negligible: cabbage, broccoli, zucchini, squash, egg plant, pepper, okra, tomato, and corn. Yet if I plant them, cultivate them, and harvest them, I have the makings of meals and a gloriously tasteful handout from nature.

In the palm of my hand the space needed, if they crowded together, would be within the circumference of a nickel. The cabbage and broccoli seeds are about the size of the period at the end of this sentence. The zucchini and squash seeds are football shaped but colorless, lifeless, and boring and need the space of a flattened aspirin. The eggplant and pepper seeds look like bits of dandruff, and if they were sprinkled on a coat collar, one would believe them to be dandruff. Okra is a basketball but a wee one with a dark dot where life resides. A tomato seed is so insignificant in looks and size it takes the faith of St. Paul to plant one. The corn is an isosceles triangle the size of a front tooth but so shriveled, wrinkled, and corpse-looking it stretches credulity to believe life lives within. But in the ground, they all come to life and have but one motive, purpose, and will: to mature and reproduce, characteristics without which gardeners would sit frustrated holding a rusted hoe.

Cabbage: it is a lamination of leaves packed fist-tight into a ball of nutrition so rich Chinese once packed a room from floor to ceiling with them in fall to help tide them over the winter. Broccoli: it's a green tree of small stature that births from its heart a collection of buds when cut produces a delightful dish. And when the parent is cut, children appear in miniature and appear again and again to succeed the parent. Zucchini: a squash green outside, off-white inside and is eaten stuffed, fried, buttered, and as an ingredient in bread. If any agency reacted as fast as it grows, there would be fewer complaints of the dead weight and moribund movement of bureaucracy.

Eggplant: it produces, if one can get it to produce, a beautiful flower and silky, pear-shaped fruit. It must be related to the potato because the potato beetle is attracted to it. Sweet and hot peppers are loyal. They grow when the weather is warm, and they continue to grow until the frost blights them. They enrich and add their unique and pungent taste to things. Okra: a pod with a thousand seeds and with parents who are models of preparation for Judgment Day. Its singularity of purpose exceeds the martyrs'. Day after day it grows and blooms, and the blossoms die, and their ovaries become seeded pods, and the pods in a few days are ripe, and the cycle continues until frost ends it. Man for his meal cuts the tender young with the nonchalance he toasts bread.

Tomato: the Marilyn Monroe of vegetables. From a hiccup of a seed comes with cultivation fruit that gives soul to a sandwich, and taste and substance to chili, spaghetti, pizza, and no end of foods. Like the beauty of a rose, its time is short once ripe. Corn: the backbone of nutrition. A grain will produce a stalk with two ears that contain a multitude of grains each of which must have a silk running from it to where it is exposed to pollen from the tassel. Corn is to the West what rice is to the East: the nutrition of a peasant and the grain of the gambler and player of markets.

Sometime in August I have at hand the products of all the seeds above-mentioned and in addition onions and garlic which I grow from sets instead of seeds. And with these products I mix a meal. I gather all the vegetables and confront them with a cutting board on which I first chop cabbage and arrange a nest so to speak in an electric skillet. Into the nest I add chopped zucchini, yellow squash, eggplant, okra, sweet peppers and hot peppers, onions, garlic, broccoli, and tomatoes. I add a half-cup of water, and over the mixture I drizzle olive oil. I place two ears of corn on the cob on top and turn the thermostat to simmer and relax. When the vegetables have slumped from steaming and most of the water has boiled off, the vegetables lie in a liquid of their juices and olive oil, and the meal is ready. For years I have kneaded and baked my bread. It doesn't shrink in the toaster and has body and texture and taste worthy of eating with the meal.

When I was younger and more active, I ladled out a healthy helping and sprinkled it liberally with shredded mozzarella, but now I am content with the helping unadorned, two ears of corn, and a slice of bread. It is a marvelously colorful meal, a meal that is a miracle and a marvel to me, for I have planted it, cultivated it, harvested it, and cooked it. It is marvelous in other respects. The meal is fresh, organic, tasty, nutritious, cheap, and satisfying. The miracle and marvel are this meal comes from such insignificant, improbable, hopeless, inarticulate, items that anyone unaware of their potential would consign to a landfill, where unbeknownst to the consignor, they would probably germinate and produce if not buried under subsequent garbage.

The miracles one reads about, such as the Lord walking on water and raising the dead, he might question. But no one who has planted that thimble full of seeds and tended those seeds to maturity doubts the miracle of seeds. The miracle of miracles is seeds dug from the graves of Pharaohs, I have read, have germinated after three thousands years of waiting for their chance of resurrection. I know first hand tomato seeds, saved and shelved for ten years, will germinate readily, grow, and produce tomatoes. Gardening is being in touch with miracles.

FALL

16

A SATURDAY AFTERNOON
IN SEPTEMBER

My work keeps me in town during the week, but on Saturday afternoons I go to the farm and enjoy myself. The joys are simple, but the adage the best things in life are free is not altogether a romantic's assessment. Some joys are free or are relatively free. Clean air is one. Rain in drought is one. Another is a blue sky populated with puffs of white and a benign sun. There are many more, and on this particular Saturday I experienced a number of them.

After providing for a night away from home, I went to the garden on the river, the garden without which I would have little to show for my efforts this summer. It weathered the drought and produced in spite of it, whereas my garden on the farm in the high country withered and produced little. I stopped to get sweet corn from a late patch, cucumbers for my dinner, and a shock or two of fodder from early corn for the cattle.

There is joy going into a garden and gathering corn, the seeds of which I planted and nurtured since the first peep of the plant to the time of tassel and the grain on the ear. I remember the patch like I remember my children: the times of worry and the times of pride, the times of cloudless skies, curled leaves, and waning hopes until rain finally comes in a clash of heat and coolness and drops life into the soil. What a relief from prolonged yearning. To a gardener the breaking of drought is not unlike the first embrace of long separated lovers.

At the farm, I unloaded and began to follow my agenda. With my ancient Gravely, I cut over a brown patch of garden gone to weed, and then with a Troy I cut the yard, resurrected by the dousing from Dennis. In the process under a pear tree I planted years ago, I found on the ground some yellow ones and came eye to eye with a ripe one on a low limb. After mowing I sat on the back steps, ate the pear, and admired the grandfather oak, heavy with acorns, spreading like a vast tent over most of the yard.

In June I had gathered accumulated packages of flowers seeds, mixed the contents in a container, and planted a row with them, advising them in parting they were on their own. At least I had given them a chance. There was enough moisture in June for them to germinate, but after the drought came, they did little but wait and pray to survive. Nevertheless, always just in time to prevent their expiration, some rain came, and then in early August two thunder storms made mud of the garden, and the plants flourished. Now, with the rain from Dennis, they have arrived.

Of all the varieties of flower seeds I planted in that row, only cosmoses and zinnias survived in abundance. A writer realizes the inadequacy of words when he tries to describe a row of flowers, but for those who are familiar with cosmoses and zinnias, a few words will do.

The cosmoses bloomed pink, purple, and white all with yellow centers and all chest high sitting atop willowy and lacy stalks. The zinnias hold their own in colors and shapes. Some are the shape of small toadstools and colored a virgin pink. One variety is wild with orange spike-like petals radiating from a brown center crowned with yellow wiggles. Standing back and taking in the whole of the row is a delight and surely one that is free. Further, both flowers produce seeds galore that can be gathered and stored for next year's planting.

I planted an apple tree about the time I planted the pear tree, and it stands near the pear. I believe the apple tree is a Jonathan. Whatever it is, it is a great apple for eating from the tree and for sauce. I find joy picking up apples from underneath it, sitting on the porch as my grandmother used to do with paring knife, preparing the apple for cooking into sauce, and eating the applesauce for breakfast. This Saturday as I have on others, I picked up the apples and prepared enough sauce to do for the week.

In the mud from Dennis I weeded the strawberry patch, a chore I would never undertake had I not had the leadership of my aunt. Never daunted, she would squat and weed the worst patches clean. This Saturday I plowed them, and now they are in good shape for the winter and spring when the berries will come barring frost and deer and drought and plague.

I fed the fodder to the cows and then sat on the back steps in view of the oak, the yard, the pear tree, apple tree, and the beautiful row of flowers, happy with it all. The afternoon by now was about gone, but I had experienced my joys, simple joys, but all the joys I need in the waning months of my seventh decade. If I live many more years, I can attribute the borrowed time to the days I have to satisfy my addiction: Saturday afternoons on the farm with a view of the hills and the trees under the sky and sun and with the opportunity to work on the land and rest on the back steps surveying my modest estate.

17

A Spring's Wake

The birds are gone except for the perennials, the canny crows and raucous jays. The leaves have fallen except for the eccentrics, victims of the earth's tilt and gravity. The golden gown of the maple lies at her feet leaving her in bare-boned nakedness. The uncertainty of a spring day is the certainty of October's. The volatility of April is the predictability of fall. Spring's fruitfulness is now spring's wake.

The gardens are brown except for the turnip crop and the strawberry patch. The tomato stakes have been pulled and stacked around the great white pine guarding the garden. The rhubarb lies stricken, slumped as if some midnight phantom had cursed it. The rose has aged in the bud and stands suspended in a limbo between death and bare breath.

Shade has migrated with the fowl of the air, and coincidentally the sun has sunk to the south, and its eye is weak. Shadows slant and for the most part are trunks of trees. A drive in evening on a sunny day through a wooded area reveals a forest of shadows of the bare boles and empty limbs of oaks and maples and the whole tree family. It's like looking through an uncurtained window.

The chestnut trees have opened their burrs and allowed their progeny to drop, reminding one of very straight-laced and prickly parents finally letting go the youth of the house. Even though the foliage is gone and the mother branches have shut down for the winter, on some apple trees the reluctant to leave still hang on. They dangle there like a hanged criminal abandoned by state and family. While sauntering, I find one and taste what summer has stored and fall has mellowed.

The daffodils have been cut over and the glads dug up. The rainbow of cosmoses and zinnias has succumbed to frost, all its glorious hues having taken leave overnight after weeks of offering its beauty to the sun.

The creeks are puddles and ponds waiting for the flow that will come, sometime. The rivers are tame and lean, all muscle and bone, having now none of that pregnant swell of spring. The eddies mirror the mountains, October's colors, and November's branches. But rivers are like sleeping dogs: a torrent can wake them into rushing madness.

October is a string of pearls: golden days and starry nights. Autumn is tranquility. A vast quietude settles in. But there is in it a hint of quiet before the storm and of a peace too good to last.

Bathed in the warmth of Indian summer, I sit in the sweet spot on my porch and survey the yard, the garden, the pasture, and the countryside. Peace and stillness are everywhere. At times I watch a leaf still hanging and note not a movement does it make. It is strangely still. The whole earth is in wake. It's a time to recall summer, contemplate fall. and gird for winter. For the seasons come and go, and all life is bent in deference to the succession of birth and death.

The days are shorter, and the nights are longer. The sun takes a short cut hugging the southern horizon. At night Venus stars on the eastern stage until the harvest moon appears. The long nights are in keeping with a wake.

I used to tag along with my aunt to sit with the dead the night long often in the dead of winter. I remember walking along wagon roads in December and looking into the heavens at the star lit sky on the way to the wake. The vastness of the heavens and the mystery of the occasion affected me so even now as I recall them I feel the uneasiness and wonder.

These days of spring's wake, I number for love of them and their sweet melancholy. Now, the spirits of the days of spring and summer gather in fall's living room where spring is laid out to exchange tales of how it was in the times of the deceased. How sad it is, but how sweet it was.

18

Where Do Butterflies Sleep?

I have a flower garden. It consists mostly of zinnias, cosmoses, and marigolds with a few calendulas. The zinnias and marigolds have proliferated. They are now in full bloom with some generations wilting and new generations budding and flowering. It is a glorious sight to see, particularly in late evening when the sun, low in the west, directs its eye point-blank at the garden. I can view it out my front window where I sit in my easy chair. It looks in the sun like a Saturday football stadium with its thousands of faces.

Among creatures enamored of the flowers are the bumblebee and the butterfly. The bumblebee in early fall finds a zinnia or marigold bloom he desires, takes up residence on it, and spends the night. His faithfulness to the flower of his choice owes more to meteorological conditions than loyalty to fidelity. This time of year the bumblebee is lethargic, so once he has found his desire, there he lies night and day. If one pokes him with a finger, the bee indicates slight irritation and resumes his fall slumber in the arms of his marigold.

The butterfly is scandalously wanton. She comes to the flowerbed flying like a top gun pilot on methadone. She soars above, wheels around and around, dives recklessly, touches down for a nano-second on an orange zinnia, speeds to another and another touching tentatively, soars again upward and over and around, dives to the flowers, skims some, and lights slightly on one. Then she finds her true interest and settles down for a long period kissing blissfully a red zinnia and imbibing its nectar. After a while she is off soaring above, wheeling this way and that, going up with the speed of a rocket, and coming down with the weight of lead to choose again some zinnia upon which to stop awhile. This is repeated until the sun has shifted its light from this garden and focused it on flowers blossoming many latitudes west of me. And then at dusk the butterfly is gone. Where does she spend the night?

Most creatures find a place to rest at night, but some creatures sleep in day and prey at night. The butterfly is a day creature. She loves the sunshine and the warmth of it. Rarely does one see her when the sky is overcast and the weather is cool. Where she stays on such days is a mystery, but the greater mystery is where she sleeps at night.

Most birds when night comes hie to trees to roost where they are safe from the daytime predators who cannot see in dark and do not hunt at night. The owl is a worrisome creature to roosting birds. They are game for the owl and for other predators that roam the dark and have sight at night and can inventory trees for meals. Chickens of the domestic kind have a domicile to enter when darkness comes. They enter it and find a roost upon which they find a place to settle down. The place a chicken roosts depends on its social position in the chickenarchy. The top rungs are for the highest in the pecking order, a place farthest above a sly fox's reach.

The squirrel finds a hole in a tree and furnishes the interior with nesting material on which he sleeps during the nights when come winds and snows and cold of winter. He also has the equivalent of a second home, a home for summer days. He collects leaves and fashions a nest in the fork of an oak miles from the ground. On summer days when he is full from nuts, he goes to the nest to dream of a fall in which no hunter fills his hide with shot and to rest and plan for his future---a future of procreation and nut-hunting, two occupations of life not unlike that of Wall Street traders.

The rabbit, the wimpiest of all animals, has her speed to protect her life. She nests like a bird on the ground, a place where jeopardy frequents more often than in tree limbs. Her nest embraces half her body. If a predator comes too close, she exits her nest with gunshot suddenness. And if pursued too closely, she takes refuge in a hole in the ground or in a rock bar. Otherwise she circles and returns to her known haunts. All life has a home.

The quail in winter get together to form a covey or family in which they cooperate in order to survive the cold and the predators. If a predator happens upon their sanctuary, there is an explosion of feathers flying, each quail going in a different direction, sailing to a random stop alone. The survivors of the intrusion gather again to nest in the night, huddled together to bring a sense of security to their lives.

The bee hies to the hive when the day's work is done. She visits hundred of flowers, inhales the nectar, returns to the hive, stores the riches she has collected, buzzes about her adventures, and then rests in a sea of honey. But the bee is bee-line oriented: no soaring up and diving down and roller-coastering joyously with a beak of intoxicating pollen. The butterfly to the bee is a wastrel, but I suspect the bee envies her delicate beauty and flights of fancy.

So where does the butterfly go when evening comes and the day goes from dusk to dark? Where does this creature, constructed with spider webs and filaments of silkworms, wings woven of cumulus clouds, sculpted by Michelangelo and painted by da Vinci---go to relax, relive the day, and dream of zinnias?

I like to think she wings to a hemlock forest shaded in day and dark at night. Her nest, formed with the gossamer of milkweed and dyed purple with the juice of elderberries, is in the fork of a hemlock where a limb leaves the trunk and touches the clouds. An outgrowth of bark serves as her canopy. The queen of flowers lies there for the night looked over by fairies and guardian angels sent by the Maker to protect this delicate, beautiful, and innocent creature, one that preys on nothing but just purloins pollen from zinnias.

When morning comes she does her toilet in a pristine spring, and when the sun comes up, she comes a-wing to my garden to dance in flight with grace from flower to flower to sip sweets.

19

Fruits from Nature

Every fall I remember my grandfather's apple orchards. In a good year he would harvest dozens of bushels of apples from them. I can remember those orchards with their weight of red and yellow apples dragging the limbs of trees to the ground, with the ground covered with dropped apples with swarms of yellow jackets and hornets feasting on them, with ladders leaning against the trees, with buckets and crates full, and finally with the crates stacked to the ceiling in the apple house, the depository of Ben Davises, Winesaps, Wolf Rivers, Grimes Goldens, Winter Rambeau, and varieties I have forgotten. And I remember standing in the doorway to the apple house smelling cider and feeling the security of that vault of wealth and thinking of hot applesauce with buttered biscuits.

Over the years I have planted many apple trees, but because I was never able to tend them as one should, my grandfather's success eluded me. But this fall two of the trees I planted twenty years ago were so abundant with fruit their limbs bent with the weight. One was a Jonathan and the other a Grimes Golden, and they outdid my dreams of an apple harvest. This spring they were an esthetic joy, both bride-white with clusters of bloom, and if every bloom had produced an apple, the trees would have split to the ground long before fall. But most of the bloom wilted and fell sterile producing no apples.

I have been picking up apples from under the Jonathan since the middle of August and cooking them into applesauce, both sweetened and unsweetened, the latter for apple butter cooking during Thanksgiving when my daughter and I have the time to make it. And I have frozen both kinds to keep until needed. I haven't had the time to can applesauce like Grandmother used to do, but it keeps well frozen and has no freezer taste even after months.

The Grimes Golden will not sauce, and, therefore, they are wonderful for making fried apples and fried apple pies. They have hung on the tree for the most part unlike the Jonathans. And on this day, a day when September had at last shouldered out August, I went to the tree and picked apples off the tree and from the ground. One on the ground was hollowed out by yellow jackets, and when I turned it over, a swarm of them panicked out just as they did when as a boy I turned over one in my grandfather's orchard. They love the sweetness of apples no less than man does and probably were in Eden under Eve's tree doing the same.

At my farmhouse with a pitcher, I dipped rainwater from one of my many rain barrels and filled the bucket of Grimes Golden to rinse them. I got a bucketful of rainwater, water as pristine clear as that in which Narcissus saw his image, and went to the kitchen and set up an assembly line to cook the Grimes Goldens into fried apples. I poured the water in the first bowl of the sink and put the apples in it. In the second bowl I put a dishpan, and on the sink drain I placed a skillet. Then with paring knife I picked up an apple, halved it, clipped out the blossom end and the stem end, quartered it, cut out the seeds and core, eighth it, put the waste in the dishpan, and the crisp slices in the skillet.

I repeated the cutting and coring until I had a skillet full of apple slices with the skin on, a skillet full of ivory and gold, to which I added a few squares of butter and helpings of brown sugar, a dash of salt, and a half cup of water. Then I applied a low heat. Soon, apple juice, butter, and brown sugar bubbled, and the crisp, white slices

transformed into limp but intact, sumptuous, somewhat translucent, caramel-covered fried apples.
When the caramelized juice reached an optimum
thickness, I turned off the heat, waited a bit, and
forked out a slice for testing. What a treat. The
toothsomeness of apple flesh and skin dripping
in thick caramel with the appropriate accompani-
ments, such as buttered biscuits, is a treat the rich
pay dearly to enjoy but which mountaineers had
often on table in season with the planting of an apple tree, a good harvest, rain water, a paring knife,
pan, and a heated skillet.

The joys of these apple trees and their progeny
and the harvest of nature's fruits are not easily
quantified. But they are riches that vie with any
credits lying dormant in bank accounts or raging
on Wall Street. I planted these trees many years
ago and transplanted them, and I have watched
them grow, fought off the deer, which love the
buds and new growth, and waited for the harvest that often didn't come but which has come
in abundance this year. Every spring I have had
the pleasure of seeing them in Eastertide bloom
and have joyed and agonized over the caprices of
weather, of just enough, of drought and deluge, of
frost and heat. There is in harvest a hearkening in
the heart to all the harvests, from time out of mind,

of which mankind has been beneficiary. It is like looking into the heaven at night or to sea in day or in the fireplace in winter.

I like the rainwater from a barrel. It is water straight from heaven, neither pumped, chlorinated, metered, or fauceted. It drops from above to roof to rain barrel to man. As well, I like to go to a tree I have long ago planted with a plan and bucket up what I dreamed of and enhance the harvest for the table. Upon terminating Adam and Eve's tenancy in the Garden, God's edict, that man should hereafter earn his living by the sweat of his brow, has not been so oppressive in reality because the apple tree and its cousins do a lot of the work and the sweating for him.

20

REMEMBERING THE APPLE HOUSE

Stealthily summer succumbs to autumn. Yesterday's light is tomorrow's dark. Day by day the light of the summer sun fades to return in the shine of the fall moons. The season of slanting shadows is slipping into place, and August's seeds are seeking a fertile nest. Foliage is tattered; grass is in seed. The purple bloom of the thistle is now gossamer, the forage of the goldfinch. The quiet here is the roar someplace. The fruits of summer are gathered, and the hay of fields is stacked. It's a time for contemplation and reminiscences, a time to retreat and seek respite from the news, and a time to find repose in the memories of former days.

On the farm there were many outhouses: the chicken house, smokehouse, the meat house, the dairy, the woodshed, the garage, the granary, the pigpen, the apple house, and others. The apple house this time of the year was like a jewelry store. Lined in shelves from floor to ceiling on one side were all the gem-like quart and pint jars

of canned fruits, vegetables, and meats preserved
and stored for mealtimes during the barrenness,
pinch, and cold of hostile winter.

Shining through the glass jars was a rainbow of
colors reflected from green beans, tomatoes, corn,
beets, pickles, and an array of reds, purples, and
blues of jams and jellies.

Jars of half-runner beans, strung and pieced,
packed in the cans helter-skelter sat beside tomatoes, skinned and quartered, with the seeds dotting
the scene like islands in a scarlet sea. Also, tomato
juice, corn relish, sweet potatoes, beets, pickles,
sausage cakes, pork loin, applesauce, grape juice,
blackberries, and everything else of spring, summer, and fall that could be preserved to tide a body
over from November to April lined the shelves.

A look at this inspired a sense of security greater
than an insurance policy issued from Connecticut.
Its beauty exceeded that of an art museum. On
the other wall of the apple house were columns of
bushel crates filled with apples and stacked from
floor to ceiling. These had come from the orchards,
a sight to see in September and October. Tree after
tree of Ben Davises, Winter Johnsons, Pearmains,
Ramboe, and others bent burdened with fruit.
Ladders rose into the trees, crates sat waiting to be
filled, and everywhere yellow jackets and hornets

sought the sweet juice. Juice of fruits is hunted and prized by all life the world around.

When the apple house was saturated, my grandfather used the surplus apples to make cider. He had a cider mill, and he recruited me to turn the handle that ground the apple into pulp that was then squeezed to produce the tart liquid. Now the fight with the bees was in earnest. No mammal in heat arouses and attracts such an army of suitors as does cider attract hives of bees. They swarm in, and they will not be denied and will drown gladly for a swill of the stuff. Nevertheless, we persevered, and cider was on the table for weeks, and in the apple house a five-gallon crock of it fermented into vinegar made to preserve whatever next season grew.

The apple house was above ground and thus was exposed to the arctic-born, bitter blasts and their prolonged sieges designed, it seemed, to frost to death all that lived.

But the apple house was a house within a house, and a foot of sawdust insulated the space between the outer house and the inner. When the tempest was fearsome, Grandmother would light a kerosene lamp and set it on a pedestal in the middle of the house to prevent the freeze from ruining the chief sustenance the family had until the crops of spring and summer matured. It worked. I have often thought somewhere sometime someone has, before the lamp, in such an emergency, lighted a candle to fight off the freeze and save the family's future. For a mere candle or lamp to be the difference between enough and too little tells a tale of how close to ruin subsistence farmers lived.

When winter came, the worn path to the apple house reflected the traffic to and from. From there came daily the makings of the meals. And a meal on a farm was no minor event where only salt was bought and hand and back, hoe, ax, and pitchfork produced what was essential. A meal was a major familial occasion. No one was absent or even late, save for sickness, at breakfast, dinner, and supper. For folks whose life was mostly work and very little play, whose entertainment in day was the bob white and in dark the whippoorwill, food loomed large as an enjoyment and a meal as a happy anticipation.

To lay aside the hoe or fork, unhitch the horse from the plow, wash up, and sit down at the family table with no knowledge of calories and cholesterol to fried potatoes, country ham, green beans, corn on the cob, apple sauce, cucumbers in cream, sliced tomatoes, hot biscuits with churned butter, whole milk, apple pie, and pound cake was as close to delirious joy as one could get. And the center and depository of the means of it all was the apple house.

The apple house is a relic replaced by the supermarket where I walk its aisles and suffer discomfort just looking because no jar I look at is known to me like the jars in the apple house. It may be happiness is producing by hand and mind what is essential to live and the use and enjoyment of it to sustain life with enough surplus to give time for rest and reflection.

21

The Fireplace

I discovered a poem titled "Those Winter Sundays" typed on an otherwise blank sheet of paper while cleaning out a drawer. I did not remember having ever read it. I did not have any knowledge of the author Robert Earl Hayden, and I don't know how I came to have it, but when I read it, I knew he and I had both experienced and benefited from "love's austere and lonely offices."

In winter on the farm in the twenties and thirties, the fireplace was---particularly in the long, dark evenings---the center around which everyone gathered. Except for a dim lamp beside the family Bible on a side table, the fireplace was the only light and the only warmth in the room. One could always find a knothole in the wall and feel winter breezing in, so the far corners, the floor, and the ceiling were cold. But before the fire and around the family it was warm and secure, and there was a sense of let winter howl and heave and do its worst. The only music was the click of the clock in time with the swing of the pendulum, the crackle of the fire, and the sigh of slumping embers.

In the fireplace was a backlog, and on the andirons was a forelog, and in between were smaller logs. The backlog was huge and lasted the night. Once its face was red with coals, one's shins knew it, and it was the backlog that supplied the banked embers for morning. The forelog and smaller logs had to be replaced frequently, so someone had to go to the porch and carry in wood from time to time, and if the supply on the porch ran out, one had to go to the woodshed to get it. When the door was opened for the carrier of logs, a wind of winter blew in with him.

Granddad stacked the woodshed with wood from ground to rafters. Some of the autumns of my youth I helped him to fill it. I would go with him with axes, crosscut saw, iron wedge, gluts made from dogwood, a maul made of hickory, and a jug of well water if no spring was near the cutting area. Granddad would choose a tree, clear the brush from around it, and cut a notch to direct its fall. Then, we would level the cross cut saw at the point of cut and begin the pull and sway, the to and fro rhythm of sawing while aromatic sawdust piled up on the ground on both sides of the cut.

Granddad would take a break to determine whether or not the cut of the saw was parallel to the cut of the notch. If it were not, we adjusted the cut to assure the hinge between tree and stump was not over cut in order to prevent an unexpected or erratic fall of the tree. Then, it was back to the rhythm and to the anticipation of the moment the tree's support began to leave it, when it began to creak and to lean ever so little and then ever so much from its upright position to an angle with the ground. The angle grew quickly, and then came a great crash and bounce and settling of the downed giant. This moment had a sad aspect to it: here lay prostrate the corpse of a live being that had been reaching for the light of sun for decades.

The brush was cut out and piled except for what was large enough to sled home. The trunk was sawed into manageable lengths, and on another day the horses were hitched to the sled, and the logs were transported to the wood yard. There on another day the hillsides would echo the whir and whine and scream of wood against the teeth of a huge wood saw by which fireplace and woodstove lengths became the final products.

I slept in an unheated room separated by a hall-way from the living room and the fireplace. By morning the only heat in the house was the fire-place's embers lying beneath inches of gray ashes. It was my grandmother who arose to Hayden's "blueblack cold" and carried a shovel of red embers to the kitchen cook stove. Her rattling the stove's grate to empty yesterday's ashes in order to start a new fire for a new day always awakened me. I would lie half awake and, as Hayden writes in the poem, hear "cold splintering and breaking," and soon after I would grab my clothes and run to the fireplace where a new blaze had risen from evening's ashes.

I don't remember ever thanking my grandmother or my grandfather, but I never spoke indifferently to them like the speaker in the poem does to his father. Nor was there ever in the house a "chronic anger" to fear. In all my days with them, they went about their "austere and lonely offices" with quiet duty and steady habits from dawn to dusk season after season. The closest they were to me was at the fireplace when winter's worst was held at bay by the heat from the blaze of the downed giants of the woods.

22

HARVESTING & HARKING
AT YEAR'S END

A few days at the end of the year were atypical. Although the nights were frosty, the daytime temperatures reached the sixties by early afternoon. On one of those days I doffed my obligations and went to the farm with the singular intention of listening to the muteness of winter and sitting on my porch looking at the pause in the glories of the place. Observing nature in December is reminiscent of sitting in a country church in midweek when all the mice have gone to town. Its glories are there, but nothing moves, nothing sounds, nothing seems animate. All is suspended, and all outdoors is sitting or standing museum-like waiting for the word from spring to wake and follow her.

I walked in the pasture toward higher ground and passed a walnut tree, not just an ordinary walnut tree but one with extraordinary girth and procreative propensity, and one that some would pay dearly to have cut and crafted into a chest or other fancy furnishing. Underneath this tree the ground was a carpet of black walnuts. The tree has produced nuts for my family for years, but this year with family gone or scattered, I had neglected to harvest any. But the proclivity to store and barn taught by those who learned lessons from squirrels prevailed. I aborted the walk and went to the house for bucket and gloves and took up the chore of nut harvesting, an occupation in harmony with nature's and Jehovah's admonishment.

I was in shirtsleeves, the sun was way to the south but benignly warm on my back, and the sky was the blue of blues, that azure infinity and eternity color the heavens. Looking east I could see forever: rolling land, pastures, farmhouse roofs, barns with cattle standing and waiting, ridges lined with trees like troops in ranks, and finally the horizon and beyond it blue that entices one to follow it to the end of time.

Amid such glories and soundlessness and under the sun's caresses, I began to squirrel away walnuts. I would roughly roll a batch of them under foot, then pick them up, remove any remaining husk, and toss the gems into a bucket. In half an hour I had nearly filled a five-gallon container, and there were tens of gallons remaining. Nature is extravagant particularly when the expenditure is to assure the perpetuity of her species. She pines not over the abortion of a thousand walnuts but rejoices over the one that germinates and becomes a tree.

At the base of the tree were the remains of a squirrel's meals over a while, a pile of shells, diamond-hard, but cut open and toothed clean of nutmeat. Here was a squirrel's Eden: ten thousand nuts and within reach a tall tree with apartments. The only risk was to be caught by a dog or other predator when too far from the apartments, but more often than not the squirrel was at the walnut tree and home before the dog awoke. To be early is the strategy of the not so strong to best the strong in the struggle.

One who has tried to crack a black walnut knows the blows necessary to open one. So when I dug up a walnut that had sprouted, I was amazed by what I discovered. A nut had opened at the seam, and from that opening was a root seeking earth and a sprout seeking the sun. With reverence and with the wish that my interruption had not been fatal, I replaced the nut and its hopes in the earth. Leaving where I had harvested I felt wealthier. I had a bucket of nuts to store until some afternoon when the sun had returned. Then, at a spot warmed by it and with hammer and stone and feasting as I worked, I could imitate the squirrel and collect a cup of kernels for cookies or cakes. I felt healthier. I could feel while bending and squatting a virtuous sensation in my legs and my back at work, not at some gym faking work, but at work at something with a needed and natural goal: harvesting against the barrenness of winter. I remembered Leo Tolstoy's first condition of human happiness: physical work under the sun and sky to fulfill a need.

I left the scene of the great tree and its progeny at its feet with my bucket of its offspring, walked to the house, and took a seat on the porch to hark to the muteness of winter and to catalogue, as it were, its museum pieces. The big maple undressed was stark in gray bark, its leafless limbs etching the blue of always. The pine still needled stood tall and forlorn, its mourning-dove nests empty. Not even a blue jay or mockingbird appeared, and the barn swallows and bluebirds were just summer memories.

By now shadows were long, and the chill of the season was seeping in. So I called it a day on the farm and with my profits returned to my obligations. How happy I am fate has seen fit to provide me with a pasture, walnut tree, and the will and time to harvest and hark. The urban man is a slave to the city and a dependent of those in the hinterlands who bring in the sheaves and edify themselves learning nature's lessons and listening to her silence.

23

A Walk in the Dead of Winter

With pictures and words of Serbs sniping at
aged Muslim mothers kneeling at the fresh graves
of soldier-sons; of Somalian children reduced to
skeletons and haunting stares by roving robbers;
of Hindus and Moslems slaughtering one another
over a plot of ground not continent enough to
bury the dead; of exiled Palestinians hovering
around campfires in Limbo; of neo-Nazis tossing
fire bombs in windows of Turkish immigrants;
and other atrocities weighing my mind, I removed
myself from civilization to rural fields and forests
for a saunter in sanity in the afternoon of the last
day of 1992.

Traffic was heavy and impatient, hurrying to be
in familiar places with familiar faces when Cinder-
ella's curfew tolled.

At my retreat the atmosphere was total tranquility: not a sign of moving life, not a sound of anything, only smoke drifting from a distant chimney
and the green sprigs and haze of the rye cover crop

of the gardens.

I walked a way that was once the highway, still identifiable as a roadbed, but now a part of the pasture. It was the county road that connected east and west and served until the thirties the migrations, trips, visits, and transportation of generations of citizens and soldiers and adventurers and school children, most of whom, like the road, were under sod. I have seen my grandmother in her seventies, as was her custom, hang up her apron, don her bonnet, and walk that dusty road a mile to get the mail and return in quick step to her chores.

The weather was out of season: a mild breeze came from the south, and a film of clouds obscured winter's weak eye, which cast faint shadows and warmed the cheeks. When the road reached high ground, the view was panoramic: miles of rolling, swelling fields and hills of forest extending to Peter's Mountain through which the New River cuts at the Narrows, a passage where for millennia man and beast trod paths.

The landscape is checkered with farms and barns. In the yards lie and stand cattle with heads up waiting for provender from their provider, at whose mercy they are, in dead of winter. A right of way for a utility beelines up and down the forest out of ken, reminding one of current weird hairdos.

The road enters a tunnel of white pines, the pines with the soft wood and velvety needles. The trees grow on both sides and reach over forming a canopy under which evidence abounds that cattle, deer, and other life find security and comfort there, shelter in winter and shade in summer.

Out of the tunnel and by the road was a barn, a bank to deposit summer's surplus against winter's pinch; a house to shelter livestock, owls, mice, swallows, groundhogs, sparrows, and bees; and a reservoir for memories of putting up hay in sweat and heat of summer and tossing it into feeding racks for hungry cattle during the snows of winter.

At the barn I saw the first life: a sparrow in a dead cedar bush. It made no sound; song is for spring. It just hopped higher and away from me, and when I walked toward it, it flew to a live cedar and disappeared in the greenery. Maybe the weighty matters of the sparrow's world had driven it also to a flight in solitude.

I left the road and entered the woods, an area too steep for cultivation but fertile for trees. It was a thicket of old-growth pines that had appeared after the hardwood had been cut and the cattle, sheep, and horses had ceased to graze it. The pines were dead or dying, and their needles and remains littered the ground and enriched the depleted soil so now the hardwoods were returning.

It was a common sight to see a maple sapling springing from the base of a moribund pine and rising cue-stick like through a labyrinth of dead limbs to its place in the sun and in future years. This reenactment of evolution's miracle of briers to oaks is the ultimate basis for optimism in a world where man's shortsightedness has made deserts of many Edens.

I reached the high ground again and looked beyond over square miles of meadows and woods with no more than a half dozen dwellings in view. After walking a mile and seeing no life but the sparrow, hearing nothing but my consciousness, I thought of scenes of rush hours in Tokyo, freeway pileups in Los Angeles, monsoons in Bangladesh, riots in India, insurrections in China, and other scenes of milling millions. I thanked whatever power granted me these moments of solitude and quietude and wondered how long it would be before those succeeding me could no longer enjoy walking a mile on New Year's Eve alone and free from the distractions of man's mad meddling.

I sat on a stump and looked about the world I was in, the land, horizon, the sky, feeling the warmth of the walk and the December sun and wondered about 1993 and the future years.

Can a nation that claims it is Christian and whose inspiration is Jesus of Nazareth reconcile its maniacal materialism with its religious aspirations and the words of its Lord: "Lay not up for yourselves treasures upon earth, where moth and rust doth corrupt and where thieves break through and steal...."? Can its heart be anywhere but where its treasure is?

Can men's and nations' fever for guns and their propensity to violence and war be cooled and curbed and the long way to peace among races, clans, tribes, and nations be advanced?

Can there be a beginning of equity in the world as to wealth, health, and opportunity? Will there be a beginning of significant reduction in population, a serious start to the end of the rapine of Earth, and a return to harmony with nature, so someone somewhere ten or a thousand years from now can still walk a pasture in tranquility and solitude with optimism?

If so, the politicians and leaders of the world must rise to new heights of talk and truth telling. They must admit the Earth is sailing the course of the Titanic; they must admit their errors and, if not reverse the course, change the tack.

24

A SEPTUAGENARIAN'S SATURDAY IN JANUARY

The last Saturday in January was a day of gold and blue and sharp shadows at noon, unmixed with the green grasses and foliage of spring and summer and uncheered with songbirds but enhanced with a whimsical wind undulating the broomsedge and whirling leaves and straws in tornadic swirls.

High pressure had moved far enough east to endow the day with south winds and benign, gate-swinging gusts from the backside of its clockwise turn. A palpable increase in the sun's treasure from six weeks ago showered its gold on meadows and hills. Just to be on the southern slope of a pasture field on such a day was glory enough, but to work there with hand and back at a basic task, warmed and cooled with sun and wind, was more than glory enough in a world where most tromped the tiles of the halls of malls and the temples of things.

I felt at home on the hillside working at a basic task because I spent many of my early days working on hillsides at basic tasks. I believed what I was doing was in harmony with nature's way and in the interest of humankind now and hereafter, regardless of how sophisticated and miraculous become the toys and trinkets of R&D and GNP. Once I began to read serious literature from Ralph Waldo Emerson and Henry Thoreau and many others who have pondered life and concluded what tasks are basic and worthy of everyman's mind and energies, I learned some fundamental values and guidance in formulating life's priorities. One such value was Thoreau's "Simplify, simplify!", a formula that in today's context is not only quaint but one lost in a wilderness of complexity.

From one book written by an author whose name escapes recall, I learned two statistics which stuck in my mind and which influence me to this day: every year this country loses more topsoil to erosion than the Japanese have to till, and it takes nature 5,000 years to create an inch of topsoil.

Without a book I deduced that the base of any civilization, the substance upon which its most magnificent creations stand, is topsoil. When the topsoil goes, all goes. When the topsoil goes, the people in the mega-cities, those whose paperworth is in billions and those on welfare and all in be-tween, will either starve or pour into the hinterland to get food by barter or force. Corn and concrete are noncompatible.

The West's wealth has come from the shameless spending of its natural legacy, that is, the mindless conversion of its soil, forest, streams, and other natural resources into forty zillion pieces of silver, a betrayal of God and nature so gross Judas's treacherous bribe-taking pales in retrospect.

It may be Adam and Eve's sin in eating the forbidden fruit dates that moment in mankind's history when man made the decision he could improve on Eden. In exchange he gave us thousands of teeming spots of pleasure and profit, and he created everywhere deserts and debris, which attest to the failure of his grandiose meddlings and miscalculations. Archeologists find ample employment spading up his mistakes.

Soil is Somalia's salvation. It is also the salvation of the hungry and starving and the source of three daily trips to the table for the rest of humankind. The number of those at the world's table is increasing in geometric progression---most of the world's five billion people having been born since 1945---while millions of tons of topsoil erode away annually. Marines, however good the few men and however high tech their equipment and transport, deliver no wheat and spare no one from starvation unless there is soil to nurture the grain.

I learned in biology soil will not sustain plant life without the residue of death, without the presence of carbon from decayed life. In nature's cycle death sustains life. This bit of knowledge caused me to visualize a cemetery of trees growing from seedlings planted in cremated remains, and it cause me to haul to my garden dead leaves, cut grass, and all organic matter in order not only to have lettuce and onions in spring but to also know philosophically the satisfaction and joy of lending a hand in nature's plan.

Thoreau said that one should build his own house and not let someone else have all the fun. He and I believe an essential ingredient of happiness is the use of one's body, mind, imagination, and creativity to provide for one's needs. Robert Frost wrote a poem telling a tale of a man splitting wood in winter when two tramps came from the woods and asked to cut his wood for pay. He was reluctant to pay others to do a job he loved. It was his play:

> *"As that I had no right to play*
> *With what was another man's work for gain.*
> *My right might be love but theirs was need.*
> *And where the two exist in twain*
> *Theirs was the better right—agreed."*

He continues with more to say about love of work and need of work:

"But yield who will to their separation,
My object in living is to unite
My avocation and my vocation
As my two eyes make one in sight.
Only where love and need are one,
And the work is play for mortal stakes,
Is the deed ever really done
For heaven and future's sake."

Thus with seventy-two years behind me, with lessons in biology, with words and thoughts of Thoreau and Frost inspiring and guiding me, and with the sun and wind my friends, I combined love and need and for future's sake shoveled cow chips into a '65 Chevy pickup and trucked the decaying carbon concentrate to the garden.

I often interrupted my labor to look to the south at the hilly horizon and take inventory of that day's blessings: the aliveness of muscles at work, the joy of pleasure with no repentance, the satisfaction of stewardship of the soil, and of maintenance of resources for millions in millenniums to come.

25

Sweet Memories of February '72

Somewhere on a shelf of home-canned foods is a pint jar with a label on the sealing lid that reads: "Maple Syrup, 2-23-72". The writing on the label is Aunt Sadie's, and the contents of the jar are the last of the syrup of our joint venture in February, 1972. Whenever a day comes in February like today, blue and gold and cold, I remember that day and all the events associated with our making of the last pint of syrup and our last joint venture in the sugar orchard.

When I was a child, my grandparents and Sadie opened the trees in the sugar orchard and introduced me to the magic and realities of making maple syrup. I can well recall 65 years later watching the sweet sap drip from elderberry spiles into hewn-poplar troughs, clay crocks, and other containers and recall as well carrying buckets of sap from the orchard through the hog lot, across a rail fence, and through the barnyard to the boiling pan where, amidst a fog of smoke and steam, I observed between trips the roiling reduction of sugar water from fifty parts to one part and enjoyed the rewarding moment when the amber syrup was lifted for straining and canning. The memory of the magic of making it and the treat of eating a glorious breakfast of buckwheat cakes, canned sausage, and maple syrup inspired me to open a few trees and make a few pints of syrup for the education of my children and the joy of a breakfast as of old.

I had in previous Februarys made a few pints by boiling sap in a large black kettle, a rather cumbersome and small-scale operation. However, in the fall of 1971 with time to spare, I planned and began a more ambitious syrup-making project for February, 1972. On a level spot at the foot of a slope on which the sugar orchard grew, I erected a shelter made of salvaged chestnut and hewn poplar logs and roofed it with tin. Under it I dug a furnace pit the shape of a johnboat, lined it with rocks, and constructed a flue at one end and a fuel opening at the other. On top of the furnace, I placed a steel pan about six feet long, three feet wide, and one foot deep and sealed it to the base with mud. With help of a Chevy pickup, I gathered firewood, downed and dry stuff, from all over the farm and hauled it to the site of operation. During the winter I had whittled spiles from elderberry limbs I had gathered from the hillsides.

My grandfather's farm was mostly hills and rocks with barely ten acres of the ninety acres level and rock free. But it was a paradise of trees, of oaks of all kinds, of straight heaven-bound poplars, of spreading chestnuts, and barrel-trunked sugar maples. One area was chestnut dominated with huge trees from which bushels of nuts covered the ground in autumn for gathering and roasting, a bounty of nature blighted and long lost. The hog lot ran to the sugar orchard, a cathedral of trees, nearly all of which were sugar maples ranging in age from fifty to two hundred years or more. The trees covered an area of about ten acres on a rocky slope, and they so shaded the acreage little underbrush grew to obstruct passage. In summer it was a sequestered island of cool and quiet; in the fall, a wonderland of yellow and red leaf. In the winter it was a vault of memories. A walk among those trees any time was a spiritual experience for me. It was my playground and my world of dreams. I would have built a cabin there for my dog and me were boyhoods longer and dreams for real.

It was there in February, 1972, that I came with containers, spiles, augers, and bit. Every tree had navel-like scars where bits had cut holes, and every tree had a stone seat at its base where containers sat in years gone, evidence of my grandparents' husbandry. I selected a spot, drilled a hole at an upward angle an inch or so deep, pushed a spile in the hole, and placed a container below it. Directly the sap began to drip. I repeated the process at other trees until eventually I opened sixty or so trees.

At the sugar camp I had two fifteen-gallon barrels in which I stored sugar water until I was ready to make syrup. I had two three-gallon milk buckets with lids that fit snugly inside the tops to prevent splashing. When the trees were running and the containers were filling, I began the rounds to collect sugar water. When I had both buckets full, I walked the paths to the camp and emptied them in the barrels or the pan. Then I walked the paths to the trees to collect more water and walked the paths back to the camp.

The collecting process was a mixture of surprise and disappointment. Every tree had a different capacity to produce sap. Some filled a container to overflowing in the same time another produced half a container. I came to know my trees, to know the ones that flowed liberally and those that dripped stingily. Some were aged and in decay with numerous scars; some were in their prime, and others were youngsters untouched by bit and spile. But all were rooted in rocks and ground under which in spring I could hear water's rushing purl, and all reached for the sun and spread their tops for its light and warmth creating an atmosphere of awe and beauty, like a church nave.

Weather determined the yield: too cold, no flow, too warm no sap for many reasons. The ideal weather was a night of stars and twenty degrees followed by a day of sun and fifty degrees. By ten o'clock on a sunny day following a freezing night, the orchard became a symphony of sights and sounds. From the icicles hanging from the spiles, tears of sap began to fall and to reflect the morning's sunrays like diamonds and to ping into pails. Suddenly the woods were filled with rays and sparkles and pings of drips, all of which had different pitches and produced a xylophone effect. It was a fairyland of sun and sounds and sights. If I could be frozen in time by some sculptor, like the figures on Keats's Grecian Urn, I would choose to be standing with buckets in hand in those sundrenched woods transfixed by the glory of sights and sounds of dripping sugar maples.

On February 23, 1972, I arrived early at the camp. I had the barrels full, and the weather was optimum for sap to run. I fired up the furnace and began to boil the sugar water I had on hand. Then

I took my buckets and started the walk into the orchard to empty the containers of the gallons of drips. By now I had a pattern of gathering and had worn paths to correspond to the pattern. I also had learned the personalities of the trees, and at every approach it was as if I were visiting a friend of long acquaintance. I emptied the proffering with thanks whether or not my expectation was exceeded. Little or lot, I was glad with what I got.

To the woods I went with empty buckets, and from the woods I returned with full buckets, six gallons a trip. Into the boiling pan I poured the sap, stoked the fire, and skimmed debris from the quieted liquid. With buckets in hand I walked again, and so it went all day: gathering sap and boiling it from fifty parts to one part.

By nine o'clock had come the magic hour and approached the critical moment when the syrup was to be removed from the fire, a moment between thin syrup and scorched syrup. This night on hand for the magic hour and moment were Aunt Sadie with her expertise to determine the precise moment of pan removal, family, and neighbors to watch the unusual sight of old-fashioned syrup making.

Stars and fire broke the dark, and the air was redolent with sweet steam and smell of syrup mixed with wood smoke. The last moments were charged with excitement, anxiety, and readiness. With much effort and pain, 150 gallons of water had been reduced to three gallons of bubbling syrup, and judgment had to be accurate to have the gain.

When the decision was made the time had come, Sadie and I lifted the pan from the furnace and placed it on logs. There in the huge pans was the sweet residue of 150 gallons and the result of twenty-five round trips to the sugar orchard, twenty that day. We dipped the syrup into a milk bucket and took it to the kitchen where Sadie strained and later canned it.

The yield was twenty-five pints, one of which still sits on a shelf as pure and sweet as it was that memorable night. When some occasion arises is worthy of the consumption of the last pint of syrup, we will open it and enjoy the essence of the sugar orchard for the last time, for the prospect maple syrup will be made there again is unlikely.

That day to this day brings joy to me even though at the end of it I was bird-dog tired. To work on a sun soaked February in maple woods, where one's ancestors worked and where every rock and tree has a memory attached, at the making of so basic a stuff as syrup; to walk the woods, to carry the sap, to chop the firewood, to breathe the clean air, to see the sparkle and to hear the music, to remember while doing; and to end the day with need for rest and with one's wages the product of his enterprise is, as they say today, to have a life. Could I have arranged my days with Aladdin's magic, I would have lived all my Februarys in that cathedral of maples working at syrup making. There, to me, is nearer to God than in the churches of stones and steeples.

26

No Mess, No Miss Bread Recipe

Since I have fifty years experience cooking and refining some recipes to blue-ribbon perfection and since there are some in the family who are aware of my culinary expertise and who fear the secrets of it might depart when I do, an event certain and now sooner than later, they have asked for one gift for Christmas: the recipe for my homemade light bread and my bread-and-butter pickles. I am glad to oblige, and I do so without any strings attached; that is, if anyone is able to convert these secrets into a commodity so sought after he or she makes a million from it, more power to him or her.

Assemble the tools: a stainless steel mixing bowl with a diameter of 16 inches and a depth of 5 inches, a sauce pan, a rubber spatula, a mixing fork or spoon, a cooling rack, three 9x5x3 bread pans, and a rolling pin.

Gather the following: 2 packages of dry yeast, 2 tablespoons of sugar, 1 tablespoon of salt, a 12 ounce can of condensed milk, 3/4 cup of shortening, about 8 cups of all-purpose flour, a tablespoon of vegetable oil, and a square of margarine or butter.

Puncture the top of the condensed milk can with a beer can opener, pour the contents into the saucepan, and fill the can with warm water. Pour the 12 ounces of warm water into the sauce pan with the 12 ounces of milk; add to the mixture the 3/4 cup of shortening, either vegetable or animal, and place the pan on medium heat.

While the pan is heating, empty the two dry yeast packages into the bowl and add the sugar and the salt. When the milk and water mixture has reached a temperature hot enough to melt the shortening but not too hot to kill the yeast (The difference is a matter of stirring the mixture and checking with your hands the temperature of the pan.), pour the mixture into the bowl and stir until thoroughly mixed. Then add two cups of flour and stir until uniform. Now add two more cups of flour and mix, and then add two more cups and mix thoroughly.

At this point the dough should be thick and sticky and resistant to easy stirring. So now is the time to change from a mixing utensil to kneading by hand, a stage somewhat critical with regards to the outcome. Clean the spoon or mixing fork with the spatula and place both of them in the saucepan. Now get the bowl to a level where you can use manual manipulations with optimum leverage and cover the dough with a cup of flour, more or less depending on the consistency of it.

If you are right-handed, grasp the edge of the bowl with the left hand, and from the flour source flour your right hand, always keeping your left hand free of dough in the event you have an irresistible urge to scratch some part of your person or lift a cup of spirits. Then begin to knead with the right hand while turning the bowl with the left hand. With experience this process is done with a rhythm: left hand turning and right hand kneading and so on.

Knead the dough and work the residue of flour at the bottom and around the edges of the bowl into the dough adding more flour if the dough becomes too sticky. Continue until the dough has become elastic and is readily shaped into a oval that is baby-bottom or baby-cheek smooth and rounded. After five minutes or so of kneading, the bowl should be fairly clean of flour, and a lump of elasticity is ready for yeast bacteria to do their work. Hold up the dough and pour a tablespoon or so of vegetable oil into the bowl and wipe the dough in the oil and place it in the bowl smooth side up. Cover with a sheet of wax paper or the equivalent and set the bowl where the temperature is optimum for rising around 70-75 degrees Fahrenheit. The temperature is somewhat critical, for if the temperature is too high, the bread will be too grainy, and if too low, it will be too lumpy.

Let the dough rise for about an hour or until it has doubled. Then on a flour board or counter top sprinkle a dusting of flour, divide the dough into three equal pieces, wipe a piece in the flour, flatten it with your hand, and get the rolling pin. Roll the piece to 1/2 inch or so thickness, first rolling the top or smooth side and then the reverse side. Roll up the dough and tuck it into a greased bread pan. Repeat with the other pieces of dough. This operation with the rolling pin, I have discovered, is critical as it gives the bread a fine texture.

Place the loaves under cover of wax paper or whatever and allow them to rise for about an hour at 70 or so degrees until the dough has pretty much filled the pans. In the meantime, set the oven temperature at 400 degrees. When the dough has risen and the oven is hot, put the three pans in the oven with a space between them and let them bake for about ten minutes. Then reduce the heat to 350 degrees and bake another ten minutes. Every oven is somewhat different, so you should check after five minutes to determine whether or not to reduce the heat sooner or later. The decision is determined by the shade of brown of the crusts.

When the bread is baked, take the pans out one at a time and after a few minutes, carefully turn them out onto a cooling rack. Take the stick of butter or margarine --butter is better -- and rub the tops of the loaves until shiny. Clean up while the bread is cooling, and then cut a slice and have a treat. Save one loaf for the table and freeze the other two for another day.

Some art is involved in the production of nearly every item of cookery. The art comes from using a recipe a number of times and learning each time the small differences that make the bread better and incorporating them from then on. Above all, when finished, step back, be proud, and reflect on bread making, a ceremony revered by all of humankind.

27

FAITH IN A GARDEN

An elderly woman who knew my passion for gardening gave me a sign inscribed: "One is nearer God's heart in a garden than anywhere else on earth." So, if in my garden I am nearer God's heart, I have such an intimate relationship with Him it should earn me divine credits, for I have been, as surely as the earth rotates, in a garden on a Sunday most Sundays of my life as well as Saturdays.

The Sunday service always begins with a survey of the garden to determine how it is progressing and what chores and sacraments to give priority. This Sunday I noted the zinnias and cosmoses were blooming vivid reds and pale purples, an exquisite entrance. The asparagus I planted in May of 2007 had sent up a crowd of sprouts too small this year for harvest but prophesying hope for next year. The cornrows were now impenetrable crowded with leaves greened with color that foretells many delicious meals of corn on the cob. A biologist's wonderment is the relationship between the tassels and the silks of a corn plant. For every grain on a corn ear there runs to it a silk whose work it is to catch a pollen from the tassel. Then, by some chemistry the grain is impregnated so it tends to swell rather than to shrivel. It is love that produces this glorious dish when just pulled then shucked, steamed, and buttered is a table's delight.

The potatoes vines were sitting on potatoes. I know for I have dug a few hills. There were tomatoes to pick and tomatoes to tie up, peppers to take, squash to collect, cucumbers to seek, and onions to pull to bind in bundles to hang in the outhouse. But the big job was picking the beans. To lift the leaves of a half-runner plant to discover a dozen or more pods containing eight to ten beans is a capitalist's dream because he had to sow one bean only to reap a hundred plus in addition to pods. So dreaming, I picked a bucketful to take home where I canned seven quarts to store away. Picking cucumbers is a hide-and-seek game. The cucumbers hide, and the pickers seek. If cucumbers were red like strawberries, the work of the picker would be easy. But they are green and of the same green as the plants. So a picker, bending and squatting under a 90-degree sun, lifts leaves to find cucumbers, and if he overlooks one, the next time he seeks he will often find a monster of a cucumber he missed two days ago.

But, I gather them. I save those of the proper size to pickle and give away those too large for pickling. Once I have enough of the proper size, I preserve them as bread-and-butter pickles from a recipe handed down from time out of mind that I have improved over the years. I add to the cucumbers sliced one-eighth inch thick, five onions thinly sliced, and five garlic buds finely chopped, and a few Hungarian hot peppers minced. The result is a product I could have made a million from had I had the entrepreneur's spirit. But, alas, I am one of those socialists who give away what they grow, subject of course to their needs to winter on.

My socialistic bent is the result of having lived on a subsistence farm during the Depression. No one around had insurance of any kind except prayers and his neighbors. I have helped to hoe a neighbor's corn, helped cut his hay, helped bring in his winter wood, split stove wood for a widow, and forked hay into a barn on a holiday when rain was imminent. Poverty induces communal living; wealth produces individualism and the philosophy of let the Devil take the hindmost. And the Devil today is involved in a burgeoning industry of taking the hindmost.

Man and woman must eat. The vulnerability of the city is if the hinterland fails to send to it what it needs to nourish it, its inhabitants panic, for they have no recourse. Concrete and blacktop will not germinate a seed. The inhabitants of a metropolis, particularly the working class, are at risk of famine and must rely on the outland farmers to furnish them food. Today the peasants of the world have crowded into cities. Mexico has now a population of thirty millions. This trend is creating a potential for catastrophe, for those who once produced the food are now with those looking for others to produce it. When there are too many to consume and too few to produce, the stress of the disproportion induces instability among other dire consequences.

Thus, I have faith in a garden. I have faith it will furnish me food and faith I am nearer to God's heart than I would be anywhere else on earth. The exercise gained in a garden is more fun than to pump iron or to treadmill on a machine. In fact, of all the win-win situations of this world, there's no more win-win than working a garden.

28

DIGGING POTATOES WITH MY GRANDSON

On the Fourth of July I had picked a half-bushel of half-runner beans before noon and had gone to the farm where my daughter, her husband, and grandson live in a renovated hundred year-old farmhouse. I went to sit on a porch with a view to string the beans. Soon, my daughter and grandson appeared to help with the beans. But stringing beans for Michael Ferrell, a thirty month-old child, was a chore he didn't work at long. So, he began to try to distract his mother by living a little dangerously here and there, and she, of course, was distraught. So, I said to my grandson, "Let's go dig potatoes." He agreed right away.

With the boy bringing up the rear, I went to the truck to get a bucket, then to the tool shed to get the hoe, and on to the garden and the potato patch. I pulled the nearly dead vines up from one hill, and one potato hung on to them. With the vines and some soil removed, a few potatoes were revealed. It was like taking a setting hen off her eggs, for

beneath those vines were a dozen potatoes of vary-
ing sizes. I took the hoe and carefully dug up the
potatoes, and Michael Ferrell picked them up and
put them in the bucket. He wanted to do the man's
job and asked for the hoe, but he soon found it too
unwieldy and gave it back to me. I gave him the
largest of the potatoes and told him to take it to his
mother. Off he went holding up the potato and telling his mother on the run he had dug a potato.

The farmhouse has been empty for twenty
years except for my visits to do some farming and
gardening, some sitting on the porch viewing,
and walking the fields and forest at first with my
children and then many times alone. I felt I was
as much a part of the land as were the groundhogs
that holed up in it and the bobwhites that nested
on it. I believed, and still do, mental health and
spiritual peace depend on closeness with nature.
The move to the farmhouse by my daughter was
to allow the boy to grow up in nature, to see the
birds and rabbits and other animals, and to walk
the fields and forests as his grandfather and mother
had before him.

Urbanites seldom are reminded they are animals
and their heritage and origin are the same as all
animals and all living things. They evolved from
simpler organisms by natural selection and existed

in nature for million of years before the advent
of the city and the great migration there. Even
though humans have left nature, nature has not left
humans, and the result is a disease one writer dubs
"nature deficit disorder."

He writes: "A lot of kids can tell you things
about the Amazon rainforest, but not many of them
can tell you the last time they lay in a field and
watched the clouds pass overhead." He deplores
the deprivation of access to and involvement in nature by children and thinks many children's disorders result from that deprivation. He would agree I
believe with the following:

Every heart divorced from the land starves. It
does so because every heart's memory is the depository of the history of life, and the history's bed
was nature and its waters, its forests, its prairies,
skies, stars, and the whole spectrum of life from
tadpole to whale and from rose to redwoods. No
man or woman can stand on the shore of a sea
and not feel nostalgia or watch a sunset and not
sense awe at its beauty or sit on a winter's evening
before a fire and not feel inordinate security. The
subconscious, within which resides eons of the
struggle of life and its moments of joy and sorrow,
is an ineradicable influence dictating acts and emo-
tions often seen as irrational relative to the envi-

ronment man has built, an environment more often than not at odds with nature's and thus with the one from which humankind emerged. The conflict between man's environment and nature's is irreconcilable and gives rise to no end of frustrations and problems for children and adults.

America's heart is starving because America has put its machines to work for it, despoiled the countryside for its ease and luxury, and destroyed it for the superfluous and the vain. In effect, it has killed its heart and soul, its immortal self, for an orgy of materialism of short duration. Mankind's remedy for its hunger has been its bane.

There is nothing more unnatural for young children than to be in a room for six hours a day. Ideally children should have the run of fields, woods, and rivers under skies and stars to learn the ways of nature and experience her beauties. This should be the lesson and orientation before any others. That it is not results in nature deficit disorders.

My daughter, her husband, and I have undertaken to assure that Michael Ferrell has the opportunity to learn the lessons and know the glories of nature. Among the lessons is that of digging potatoes. The garden I have planted is part of his playground, and I hope someday a garden will be his recreation if not his occupation.

29

A Commencement Address: The High Road to Happiness

Greetings, fellow students and fellow members of the faculty. I say fellow because I have been both a student and a teacher. I have sat in a classroom to learn, and I have stood in a classroom to teach. I have been there and done that, as the saying goes.

I stand before you a happy man; at least, I am happy today. I am cautious because I remember the story of the king who had a world of happiness one day and a world of misery the next. I am happy because I have excellent health for a man who is 90. I am educated and have a profession. I have served my country. I have no debts, and I have sufficient credits to see me through to the end, perhaps. I have a doting daughter who is a lawyer, and an admiring son who is a professor. And I have a grandson who has the makings of a Greek god. I experience remorse but none crippling of mind; I have regrets but none that burden me.

I have loved and lost and loved and had it requited. I have a place where I can climb to a mountaintop and see its peers: one in the west and one in the east. From there I have seen the moon rise and sun set simultaneously. And I have gardens, and I cultivate them, preserve the products of them, and sit at table to dine on them.

However, I have not always been happy. In fact, there have been times when I have suffered such despair and mental misery I contemplated ending my life. What stayed my hand was the image of the horror on my daughter's face upon discovering what I had done.

I am a manic-depressive victim. In the manic stage I had a talent for quips, and in the depressive stage I was all but in a catatonic condition. In the manic stage I would commit myself to challenging initiatives, and when the depression came, I suffered not only from the depression but also from the guilt of not carrying the responsibilities of the initiatives. Finally, the fear of being undercut by depression when I was pursuing some dream inhibited my pursuit of it. In a sense the disease was a blessing in disguise, for had I not had such a disabling affliction, I would probably not be as happy a man as I am. I may have gone to the city and run with the big dogs, a decision I see now as a disaster for me.

To what do I attribute my current happiness?

From my experiences and from the books I have read and the thinking I have done, what can I tell you to do to find happiness? I will begin with Leo Tolstoy's five conditions for human happiness. His first was we must live close to nature, live under the sun and stars and in fields and forest. We must work at something we are fond of, and the work must be needed and physical so as to give us an appetite and sound restful sleep. We must have a family conceived for the love and the joy of it. We must have amicable dialog with all the different people of the world. And we must die a healthy and painless death, a death that comes after years of healthful living near nature in a natural environment.

Society can be divided between those who pay interest and those who receive interest. Join those who receive interest as soon as you can or at least join those who do not pay or receive it. You must never borrow yourself into a financial hole from which you can never escape. Save and scrape and do with little, so in the long run you can have much. Follow the advice of the Greek philosopher Diogenes who advised one should reduce one's wants rather than work to satisfy his wants, which are endless. If you die before the saving pays off, what difference will it make? Above all, take care of your health, for when it goes, it all goes, just as when the roof goes, the house goes. And this: learn to live peacefully with yourself, for if you do not, you may become your worst enemy.

The use of leisure time is critical as to whether you succeed in life. If you use your leisure to advance yourself by reading, walking, gardening, writing, thinking, studying, attending uplifting entertainment, listening to wiser heads, you will profit. If you use it to indulge yourself in those activities and things detrimental to your body and mind and empty your pockets, you are likely to fail and never know happiness except during those moments of indulgence. I don't suggest you become an anchorite or a monk but become a person who is moderate in all things.

Do not take another's word for anything without examining it. Particularly, scrutinize what your parents have taught you and expose their teachings to reason, experience, and logic, and if you come to another conclusion, forsake the teaching. Leave the parental haven and the haven of those in loco parentis and sail the seas of doubt until you have fashioned a haven of your own, a haven that is tentative, always that is tentative.

Be aware man lives in a world of illusions. He first thought the earth was flat and the center of the universe, a god created all that exists in days, and everyone has an eternal soul and a free will. It just may be, of which convincing evidence exists, evolution created Homo Sapiens and all else. And it may be true no one has an eternal soul or has free will, and the belief in them is illusionary.

Never make decisions on the premise first love or second love will last forever. Never make decisions what is now will be here tomorrow. Never believe you will reach a plateau of happiness that will exist forever. Never believe getting and spending is the way to eternal happiness. Never forget you are a product of nature; she is your mother and she has fashioned you and incorporated within your genes certain mandates you are to obey or suffer consequences if you do not.

Lastly, if you marry and have children, stay with the union if you possibly can, for there is no pain for the parents and for the children like the pain of parents divorced. I know. I have been there and done that also.

Finally, may the fates be kind to you, for it is the fates that determine to a very large extent, if not exclusively, what your life will be like, whether or not you will be happy or miserable, or live in the land of limbo. What I have spoken is a synopsis of what I have learned in 90 years. I hope it helps you in your quest for happiness. Good luck and goodbye.

30

Now Turned to Green Shoot

One learns in biology earth without decayed matter will not sustain plant growth, and since animal growth is dependent upon plant growth, then earth that contains not death will not sustain any kind of life. I recalled learning earlier in school that American Indians put a fish in the hill of corn to fertilize the corn. And the logic of that led to the question of why not put a human corpse in a hill of an apple tree or an oak to fertilize it. I posed this question to myself, for I knew enough of the world not to shock it with such a suggestion.

The Egyptians disposed of royal corpses by mummification at enormous expense of human labor to build mausoleums to house the preserved remains. How ridiculous, how wasteful, how unnatural, I thought, to move mountains, so to speak, to bury a body that by nature's mandate should be better planted at the foot of tree to decay and then to rise to its leaves or in a rose garden to color a bloom.

Then, of course, it occurred to me man today does just the same as the Egyptians and their predecessors did thousands of years ago. He still mummifies the body of the dead, still encases it in a costly coffin, wraps that in a water-proof copper container, and maybe that in an earthquake-proof mausoleum not a pyramid, but certainly an imitation. And then he leaves this monstrosity to nature for her to digest and resolve it all to a natural state eventually getting to the remains to put them back into circulation. How frustrated Mother Nature must be by all these funereal obstacles to her cosmic conversions.

Why have hillside cemeteries with their Hong Kong flowers coloring them with the good land loaded with granite quarried in Vermont, when a better way would be to cremate the dead and deposit the remains where a tree is simultaneously planted? Thus, in time there would be a forest or an orchard or both. And the dead would be living, and the living would be shaded and nurtured by them. In this manner man could for once be working in harmony with nature instead at odds with her. And to work with nature instead of against her is surely a proposition worthy of consideration, particularly when by such partnership one gone can soon return to life in any number of living varieties.

Lately, I learned to my utter delight this concept I had so long pretty much kept to myself was conceived a century ago by Thomas Hardy, my frequent companion and source of solace, and put to poetry:

Transformations
Portions of this yew
Is a man my grandsire knew,
Bosomed here at its foot:
This branch may be his wife,
A ruddy human life
Now turned to green shoot.

These grasses must be made
Of her who often prayed,
Last century, for repose;
And the fair girl long ago
Whom I often tried to know
May be entering this rose.

So, they are not underground,
But as nerves and veins abound
In the growths of upper air,
And they feel the sun and rain,
And the energy again
That made them what they were!

When I consider all the emotional, commercial, and religious voices that would howl in opposition to my views and proposals regarding the disposition of corpses, I concede the irrational method now employed will continue another thousand years without major change, even though the price of conventional disposal of the dead now is an amount third to house and car.

Yet, fortunately, as of now at least, I can direct the manner of the disposition of my remains however I see fit with reasonable certainty the manner will be honored, so long as it violates no law, of course. And I have directed every one who might have a say the way in which nature gets my spent self.

Ashes to ashes and dust to dust will literally be the manner. Cremation is the only sensible method of disposition. All rot is slow fire. So, why not speed the rotting up and have in a pot the residue to place, plant, and pour wherever one has in life picked out? Why not have the choice to return soon to a green shoot of one's favorite plant or to grass where cattle graze or to a rose garden to redden more brightly the bud of one.

Graves are forgotten and abandoned, memories fade and go blank, and the dead sooner or later move into the past's abyss beyond memory, care, or concern of the folk who follow. So memorials are in the long run doomed to debris. But so long as the sun comes up, the chances are great plants and trees will thrive, and those long gone will reside in one or more of them, and such an eventuality is monument and immortality enough.

Then, one can point to a tree at random and say with some credibility: "Portion of this yew / Is a man my grandsire knew."